Academic Encounters

2nd Edition

Kim Sanabria
Carlos Sanabria
Series Editor: Bernard Seal

American Studies 2

LISTENING

SPEAKING

D1599559

CAMBRIDGE
UNIVERSITY PRESS

CAMBRIDGE
UNIVERSITY PRESS

32 Avenue of the Americas, New York, NY 10013-2473, USA

Cambridge University Press is part of the University of Cambridge.

It furthers the University's mission by disseminating knowledge in the pursuit of education, learning and research at the highest international levels of excellence.

www.cambridge.org
Information on this title: www.cambridge.org/9781107688834

First published 1999
Second edition 2013
3rd printing 2014

Printed in the United States of America

A catalog record for this publication is available from the British Library.

ISBN 978-1-107-62547-1 Student's Book with DVD
ISBN 978-1-107-68883-4 Teacher's Manual

Additional resources for this publication at www.cambridge.org/academicencounters

Layout services: NETS, Bloomfield, CT

Table of Contents

Scope & Sequence   4

Introduction   8

Student Book Answer Keys   16

Lecture Quizzes   39

Lecture Quiz Answer Keys   47

Audio Script   50

Scope and Sequence

Unit 1: Laws of the Land • 1

Content	L Listening Skills	S Speaking Skills
Chapter 1 **The Foundations of Government** page 3	**Interview 1** Reasons for Voting or Not Voting **Interview 2** Voter Turnout **Lecture** The Structure of the U.S. Federal Government	Listening for different ways of saying *yes* and *no* Listening for tone of voice Listening for main ideas Listening for the plan of a lecture	Previewing the topic Examining graphics Retelling what you have heard Sharing your opinion Asking and answering questions Sharing your knowledge
Chapter 2 **Constitutional Issues Today** page 19	**Interview 1** Important Constitutional Rights **Interview 2** A Controversial Right **Lecture** The First Amendment	Listening for specific information Listening for stressed words Listening for main ideas and details	Sharing your opinion Previewing the topic Understanding humor about the topic Role-playing Predicting what you will hear

Unit 2: A Diverse Nation • 41

Content	L Listening Skills	S Speaking Skills
Chapter 3 **The Origins of Diversity** page 43	**Interview 1** Immigration to the United States in the 1860s **Interview 2** Immigration to the United States in the 1900s **Lecture** Immigration to the America: Challenges and Contributions	Listening for numerical information Listening for tone of voice Listening for specific information Listening for transitional phrases that introduce supporting details Using telegraphic language	Examining graphics Answering true/false questions Retelling what you have heard Applying what you have learned Conducting research Answering multiple-choice questions Personalizing the topic
Chapter 4 **Diversity in the United States Today** page 62	**Interview 1** Reasons for Coming to the United States **Interview 2** Adapting to Life in the United States **Lecture** Recent Immigrants and Today's United States	Listening for percentages and fractions Listening for specific information Listening for stressed words Listening for definitions	Sharing your opinion Discussing your experience Previewing the topic

V Vocabulary Skills	N Note Taking Skills	Learning Outcomes
Reading and thinking about the topic Building background knowledge on the topic Building background knowledge and vocabulary Examining vocabulary in context Guessing vocabulary from context	Using information the lecturer puts on the board Taking good lecture notes	Prepare and deliver an oral presentation on an American president
Reading and thinking about the topic Examining vocabulary in context Guessing vocabulary from context	Understanding numbers, dates, and time expressions Using symbols and abbreviations Using a map to organize your notes Conducting a survey	

V Vocabulary Skills	N Note Taking Skills	Learning Outcomes
Reading and thinking about the topic Building background knowledge on the topic Examining vocabulary in context Guessing vocabulary from context	Taking notes on handouts Organizing your notes in columns	Prepare and deliver an oral presentation in pairs on an interview conducted outside of class
Reading and thinking about the topic Building background knowledge on the topic Examining vocabulary in context Guessing vocabulary from context	Reviewing and revising notes Using bullets to organize your notes	

Unit 3: **The Struggle for Equality** • 83

	Content	**L** Listening Skills	**S** Speaking Skills
Chapter 5 **The Struggle Begins** page 85	**Interview 1** A Personal Encounter with Segregation **Interview 2** An Inspiring Time **Lecture** The Civil Rights Movement and the Women's Movement	Listening for answers to *Wh-* questions Listening for specific information Listening for stressed words Listening for guided questions	Sharing your opinion Drawing inferences Reviewing your notes after a lecture
Chapter 6 **The Struggle Continues** page 102	**Interview 1** Issues of Inequality **Interview 2** Working with the Blind **Lecture** Two Important Laws in the Struggle for Equality	Listening for specific information Listening for main ideas Listening for tone of voice Listening for signal words and phrases	Thinking critically about the topic Sharing your opinion

Unit 4: **American Values** • 125

	Content	**L** Listening Skills	**S** Speaking Skills
Chapter 7 **American Values from the Past** page 127	**Interview 1** Personal Values **Interview 2** Values in Theory and Practice **Lecture** Three American Folk Heroes	Listening for specific information Listening for tone of voice Listening for main ideas Listening for key words	Sharing your opinion Answering true/false questions Sharing your knowledge
Chapter 8 **American Values Today** page 143	**Interview 1** Differences in Values Between Parents and Children **Interview 2** Values in the Workplace **Lecture** Conservative and Liberal Values in American Politics	Listening for specific information Listening for stressed words Listening for general statements	Sharing your knowledge Sharing your opinion Drawing inferences Role-playing Conducting a survey

V Vocabulary Skills	N Note Taking Skills	Learning Outcomes
Reading and thinking about the topic Building background knowledge on the topic Examining vocabulary in context Guessing vocabulary from context	Creating your own symbols and abbreviations Organizing your notes in a chart	Prepare and deliver a poster presentation on an individual who played a role in the struggle for equality
Reading and thinking about the topic Building background knowledge on the topic Examining vocabulary in context Guessing vocabulary from context	Indenting Using an outline Using your notes to make a time line	

V Vocabulary Skills	N Note Taking Skills	Learning Outcomes
Reading and thinking about the topic Building background knowledge on the topic Examining vocabulary in context Guessing vocabulary from context	Clarifying your notes Taking notes on questions and answers	Prepare and deliver an oral presentation on a value you consider important
Reading and thinking about the topic Examining vocabulary in context Building background knowledge on the topic Guessing vocabulary from context	Taking notes in a point-by-point format Using information on the board to help you take notes	

Introduction

The *Academic Encounters* Series

Academic Encounters is a sustained content-based series for English language learners preparing to study college-level subject matter in English. The goal of the series is to expose students to the types of texts and tasks that they will encounter in their academic course work and provide them with the skills to be successful when that encounter occurs.

At each level in the series, there are two thematically paired books. One is an academic reading and writing skills book, in which students encounter readings that are based on authentic academic texts. In this book, students are given the skills to understand texts and respond to them in writing. The reading and writing book is paired with an academic listening and speaking skills book, in which students encounter discussion and lecture material specially prepared by experts in their field. In this book, students learn how to take notes from a lecture, participate in discussions, and prepare short presentations.

The books at each level may be used as stand-alone reading and writing books or listening and speaking books. Or they may be used together to create a complete four-skills course. This is made possible because the content of each book at each level is very closely related. Each unit and chapter, for example, has the same title and deals with similar content, so that teachers can easily focus on different skills, but the same content, as they toggle from one book to the other. Additionally, if the books are taught together, when students are presented with the culminating unit writing or speaking assignment, they will have a rich and varied supply of reading and lecture material to draw on.

A sustained content-based approach

The *Academic Encounters* series adopts a sustained content-based approach, which means that at each level in the series students study subject matter from one or two related academic content areas. There are two major advantages gained by students who study with materials that adopt this approach.

- Because all the subject matter in each book is related to a particular academic discipline, concepts and language tend to recur. This has a major facilitating effect. As students progress through the course, what at first seemed challenging feels more and more accessible. Students thus gain confidence and begin to feel that academic study in English is not as overwhelming a task as they might at first have thought.

- The second major advantage in studying in a sustained content-based approach is that students actually gain some in-depth knowledge of a particular subject area. In other content-based series, in which units go from one academic discipline to another, students' knowledge of any one subject area is inevitably superficial. However, after studying a level of *Academic Encounters* students may feel that they have sufficiently good grounding in the subject area that they may decide to move on to study the academic subject area in a mainstream class, perhaps fulfilling one of their general education requirements.

The four levels in the series

The *Academic Encounters* series consists of four pairs of books designed for four levels of student proficiency. Each pair of books focuses on one or more related academic subject areas commonly taught in college-level courses.

- *Academic Encounters* 1: The Natural World
  Level 1 in the series focuses on earth science and biology. The books are designed for students at the low-intermediate level.

- *Academic Encounters* 2: American Studies
  Level 2 in the series focuses on American history, politics, government, and culture. The books are designed for students at the intermediate level.
- *Academic Encounters* 3: Life in Society
  Level 3 in the series focuses on sociological topics. The books are designed for students at the high-intermediate level.
- *Academic Encounters* 4: Human Behavior
  Level 4 in the series focuses on psychology and human communication. The books are designed for students at the low-advanced to advanced level.

New in the Second Edition

The second edition of the *Academic Encounters* series retains the major hallmark of the series: the sustained content approach with closely related pairs of books at each level. However, lessons learned over the years in which *Academic Encounters* has been on the market have been heeded in the publication of this brand new edition. As a result, the second edition marks many notable improvements that will make the series even more attractive to the teacher who wants to fully prepare his or her students to undertake academic studies in English.

New in the series

Four units, eight chapters per level. The number of units and chapters in each level has been reduced from five units / ten chapters in the first edition to four units / eight chapters in the second edition. This reduction in source material will enable instructors to more easily cover the material in each book.

Increased scaffolding. While the amount of reading and listening material that students have to engage with has been reduced, there has been an increase in the number of tasks that help students access the source material, including a greater number of tasks that focus on the linguistic features of the source material.

Academic Vocabulary. In both the reading and writing and the listening and speaking books, there are tasks that now draw students' attention to the academic vocabulary that is embedded in the readings and lectures, including a focus on the Academic Word list (AWL). All the AWL words encountered during the readings and lectures are also listed in an appendix at the back of each book.

Full color new design. A number of features have been added to the design, not only to make the series more attractive, but more importantly to make the material easier to navigate. Each task is coded so that teachers and students can see at a glance what skill is being developed. In addition, the end-of-unit writing skill and speaking skill sections are set off in colored pages that make them easy to find.

New in the reading and writing books

More writing skill development. In the first edition of *Academic Encounters*, the reading and writing books focused primarily on reading skills. In the second edition, the two skills are much more evenly weighted, making these books truly reading and writing books.

End-of-chapter and unit writing assignments. At the end of each chapter and unit, students are taught about aspects of academic writing and given writing assignments. Step-by step scaffolding is provided in these sections to ensure that students draw on the content, skills, and language they studied in the unit; and can successfully complete the assignments.

New and updated readings. Because many of the readings in the series are drawn from actual discipline-specific academic textbooks, recent editions of those textbooks have been used to update and replace readings.

New in the listening and speaking books

More speaking skill development. In the first edition of *Academic Encounters*, the listening and speaking books focused primarily on listening skills. In the second edition, the two skills in each of the books are more evenly weighted.

End-of-unit assignments. Each unit concludes with a review of the academic vocabulary introduced in the unit, a topic review designed to elicit the new vocabulary, and an oral presentation related to the unit topics, which includes step-by-step guidelines in researching, preparing, and giving different types of oral presentations.

New and updated lectures and interviews. Because the material presented in the interviews and lectures often deals with current issues, some material has been updated or replaced to keep it interesting and relevant for today's students.

Video of the lectures. In addition to audio CDs that contain all the listening material in the listening and speaking books, the series now contains video material showing the lectures being delivered. These lectures are on DVD and are packaged in the back of the Student Books.

The *Academic Encounters* Listening and Speaking Books

Skills

The *Academic Encounters* listening and speaking books have two main goals. The first is to help students develop the listening and note taking skills needed to succeed in academic lecture settings. The second goal is to help students build confidence in their speaking ability – in casual conversation, classroom discussion, and formal oral presentations.

To this end, tasks in the *Academic Encounters* listening and speaking books are color-coded and labeled as L ⓛ Listening Skill tasks, V ⓥ Vocabulary Skill tasks, S ⓢ Speaking Skill tasks, and N ⓝ Note Taking Skill tasks. At the beginning of each unit, all the skills taught in the unit are listed in a chart for easy reference.

- **Listening Skills ⓛ.** The listening skill tasks are designed to promote success in a variety of listening contexts, from brief instructions to extended academic lectures, and for a wide range of purposes including listening for specific details, identifying general ideas, and evaluating extra-linguistic features such as tone of voice.

- **Vocabulary Skills ⓥ.** Vocabulary learning is an essential part of improving one's ability to understand spoken language, especially in an academic setting. It is also key to oral expression. Pre-listening vocabulary tasks throughout the book provide context for interviews and lectures. Exercises stress the importance of guessing from context. Oral activities also include suggested words and expressions. Each end-of-unit review features both a written and oral academic vocabulary review activity to reinforce the academic words that have been introduced.

- **Speaking Skills ⓢ.** The speaking skills exercises in the book are designed to introduce and facilitate the practice of language and communication skills that students will need to feel comfortable in casual social contexts as well as academic settings. They range from presenting personal opinions to conducting an interview. Language models are provided.

- **Note Taking Skills ⓝ.** Lecture note taking is key to academic success, and is thus a major focus of the *Academic Encounters* listening and speaking books. In each chapter, the lecture section introduces a specific aspect of note taking, providing a focus for listening to the lecture itself and for follow-up comprehension checks. Additional non-academic note taking skills are practiced throughout each chapter and frequently "recycled" for maximum practice.

The audio program

Authentic listening material, based on real interviews and lectures, forms the basis of the chapter material. Each chapter includes a warm-up listening exercise to introduce the topic, informal interviews that explore different aspects of the topic, and a two-part academic lecture on related material. These different types of listening expose students to varied styles of discourse, and they all recycle the chapter's concepts and vocabulary.

The complete audio program is available on audio CDs. In addition, a DVD containing the lecture delivered by a lecturer in front of a classroom is included in the back of the *Student Book*. Transcripts of the lectures are also provided in the back of the *Student Book* and the complete transcript of all this listening material is included in this *Teacher's Manual*.

Tasks

Whenever a task type occurs for the first time in the book, it is introduced in a colored commentary box that explains what skill is being practiced and why it is important. At the back of the book, there is an alphabetized index of all the skills covered in the tasks.

Order of units

The units do not have to be taught in the order in which they appear, although this is generally recommended since tasks increase in complexity, and because note taking tasks may draw on skills originally presented in an earlier chapter. However, teachers who wish to use the material in a different order may consult the scope and sequence in the front of the *Student Book* or the Skills Index at the back of the *Student Book* to see the information that has been presented in earlier units.

Course length

Each chapter in the *Academic Encounters* listening and speaking books represents approximately 10 hours of classroom material. The new end-of-unit activities may take an additional 3 hours of class time. Multiple opportunities exist to lengthen the course by the addition of related material, longer oral presentations, movies, debates, and guest speakers on the chapter topics. However, the course may also be made shorter. Teachers might choose not to do every task in the book and to assign some tasks as homework, rather than do them in class.

Quizzes

The *Academic Encounters* series adopts a sustained content-based approach in which students experience what it is like to study an academic discipline in an English-medium instruction environment. In such classes, students are held accountable for learning the content of the course by the administering of tests.

In the *Academic Encounters* series, we also believe that students should go back and study the content of the book and prepare for a test. This review of the material in the books simulates the college learning experience, and makes students review the language and content that they have studied.

At the back of this *Teacher's Manual* are eight reproducible lecture quizzes containing short-answer questions. Students should complete these quizzes after they listen to the lecture and do all related exercises.

General Teaching Guidelines

In this section, we give some very general instructions for teaching the following elements that occur in each unit of the *Academic Encounters* listening and speaking books:

- The unit opener, which contains a preview of the unit content, skills, and learning outcomes
- The *Getting Started* sections, which help students prepare for the chapter topic
- The *Real-Life Voices*, which are short interviews with people of all ages and backgrounds on the chapter topic the chapter topic
- The *In Your Own Voice* sections, which provide students with an opportunity to discuss their own opinions on the topic
- The *Lectures*, which are at the end of each chapter
- The *Unit Review* activities, which include vocabulary reviews and an oral presentation. These are included at the end of each unit

Unit Opener

The opening page of the unit contains the title of the unit, a photograph related to the content of the unit, and a brief paragraph that summarizes the unit. Have the students discuss what the title means. Have them look at the art on the page, describe it, and talk about how it might relate to the title. Read the paragraph summarizing the unit contents as a class, making sure that students understand the vocabulary and key concepts. At this point it is not necessary to introduce the unit topics in any depth.

The second page lists the unit contents: the titles of the two chapters within the unit and the titles of the interviews and lecture in each of the two chapters. Have students read the titles and check for understanding.

After reviewing the contents, have students focus on the listening, speaking, vocabulary, and note taking skills that they will be practicing in the unit. Ask students if they recognize any of the skills listed. It is not necessary for them to understand all of the terms used at this point, since the skills will be introduced and explained when they appear in the unit. Finally, go over the *Learning Outcomes*. Explain to students that the subject matter and the language skills that they will be learning throughout the unit will help them prepare for this final oral presentation.

The unit opener section should take less than an hour of class time.

Getting Started

This section contains material that is designed to activate students' prior knowledge about the topic, provide them with general concepts or vocabulary, and stimulate their interest. The section begins with a photograph, cartoon, or image. Have students look at the image and read the questions about it. Here and throughout, maximize opportunities for students to develop oral fluency and confidence by having them answer and discuss in pairs or small groups before reviewing as a class.

A short reading related to the chapter topic follows. Have students read and then respond orally to the comprehension and discussion questions that follow. The questions are designed to go beyond the reading and elicit language and concepts that will be presented in the chapter, so encourage students to volunteer their own information and ideas.

An introductory listening activity concludes this section. The type of listening task is determined by the chapter content. It may involve completing a chart, doing a matching exercise, or listening for specific information. The task provides skill-building practice and also gives students listening warm-up on the chapter topic. Make sure that students understand what is expected of them before they listen, and replay as needed so that all students feel successful. The follow-up comprehension and discussion questions can be answered as a class, in pairs, or in small groups.

The *Getting Started* section should take about one hour of class time.

Real-Life Voices

Real-Life Voices, which contains one or more informal interviews on topics related to the chapter content, is divided into three sub-sections:

Before the Interview(s)

This sub-section contains a pre-listening task that calls on students either to predict the content of the interview or to share what they already know about the topic from their personal or cultural experience. Be sure to take enough time with this task for all students to contribute. Students can also benefit here from each other's background knowledge.

Interview(s)

Because unfamiliar vocabulary is a great stumbling block to comprehension, each listening activity is preceded by a glossed list of terms (many of them colloquial) that will be heard in the interview. Have students review the vocabulary.

The next task prepares students to understand the content of the interview excerpt that they will hear; a variety of task types are used, including true-false statements, incomplete summaries, and short-answer questions. Have students review this task carefully as it will help them focus on the pertinent information as they listen to the interview excerpt.

After they have listened to all of the interview(s) and checked their comprehension, an additional listening exercise directs the students' attention to a specific aspect of language use featured in the interview(s), such as verb tense or tone of voice.

After the interview(s)

This sub-section provides students with activities to demonstrate and deepen their understanding of the concepts presented in the interviews. It may involve synthesizing information from a short reading or drawing inferences about material in the interviews. Encourage all students to contribute their opinions.

The *Real-Life Voices* section should take three to four hours of class time.

In Your Own Voice

This section builds on the content presented up to this point in the chapter and also focuses on one or more language functions (for example, asking for opinions, expressing interest, expressing polite negatives) that either were used in the *Real-Life Voices* interviews or are relevant to discussion of the chapter topics. Semi-structured speaking activities elicit the functional language, relate to the chapter content, and encourage students to share their own information. Language examples are given. Allow students to practice the language with a number of partners, and perform for the class if they like. The focus is on developing confidence with the functional language required for casual conversation and discussion.

The *In Your Own Voice* section should take approximately one hour of class time.

Academic Listening and Note Taking

This section, which is constructed around a recording of an authentic academic lecture, is divided into three sub-sections:

Before the Lecture

This sub-section begins with a brief introduction of the lecture topic and the person who is giving the lecture. Read it as a class and ask students about any language that is unfamiliar. Encourage students to guess at the meaning of unfamiliar words.

The following task either provides background information on the lecture or elicits what students may already know about the lecture topic. Topics in the book are chosen to be of general interest, so encourage that interest in students by asking them to volunteer what they already know. Some students will likely have studied the lecture material in their first language; let them become the experts in providing context for their classmates.

Finally, this sub-section introduces a specific academic note taking skill that is determined by the language of the lecture itself and sequenced to build on skills studied in previous chapters. A language box explains the skill in detail. Go over this explanation as a class and answer any questions. The sub-section concludes with a short listening activity featuring lecture excerpts that focus on the specific note taking skill.

Lecture

Each lecture is divided into two parts, for ease of comprehension. Before they listen, students complete a vocabulary exercise that focuses on the academic vocabulary in the lecture that is likely to be unfamiliar. The vocabulary is presented in the context in which students will hear it; encourage them to guess at the meaning.

Following the vocabulary task, students preview a comprehension task designed to provide a framework for their listening and note taking. The task may involve completing a summary or outline, or answering comprehension questions. Then, students listen to the lecture itself, practicing the note taking skills they have learned. Make it clear to students that for most of the lecture comprehension tasks, their answers need not be word-for-word the same. Encourage them to paraphrase.

After the Lecture

This sub-section invites students to share their perspective through discussion questions that allow them to analyze the chapter content more critically, often by comparing it to new written or graphic material. Students may be asked to apply what they have learned to their own situations. As with other discussion activities included throughout the chapter, this activity will help students prepare for the final oral presentation in two ways: they will develop oral skills and confidence, and they will identify what aspects of the unit content they are most interested in exploring further.

The *Academic Listening and Note Taking* section should take about four or five hours.

Unit Review

This section includes a review of academic vocabulary and unit topics, and culminates in an oral presentation:

Academic Vocabulary Review

The *Academic Vocabulary Review* can be done in class or as homework. As with all vocabulary activities in the book, it stresses the importance of context. As you review the vocabulary words, ask students to recall the context in which they learned them. If a word has been used to mean different things in different chapters (for example, "depressed"), elicit that information as well.

A second vocabulary review activity asks students to answer questions about the unit content; relevant vocabulary words are provided. This activity may be done orally in pairs or small groups. Students may then volunteer sentences to be written on the board, providing a class review of the unit.

Oral Presentation

Each of the unit reviews concludes with a different type of oral presentation. Carefully scaffolded activities, presented in three steps, encourage students to work on oral delivery:

- *Before the Presentation*
- *During the Presentation*
- *After the Presentation*

Before they make their presentations, students are generally instructed to choose or define a topic they will discuss. They may be asked to present to a small or large group, individually or in a team. The organization of the presentation depends on the parameters established in each chapter, but students may be asked to research their topic online or study language related to introducing or structuring a topic. Instructors should monitor the students' choice of topic and make sure they understand how best to structure their allotted time.

The *During the Presentation* section instructs students about speaking clearly, taking time to define new words, using appropriate body language, and other mechanisms for making effective presentations. This is the students' chance to work on their oral delivery and make sure that the audience understands their presentation. This is the instructor's chance to work on oral delivery skills.

After the presentation, students learn to check that their listeners have understood their presentation. They learn language to check for comprehension, engage in self-assessment, and learn how to respond to others' presentations with questions and comments.

The *Unit Review* should take three to four hours of class time, depending on the number of students in the class and the time that instructors decide to dedicate to this activity.

Chapter 1
The Foundations of Government

1 Getting Started

1 Reading and thinking about the topic Page 4
B

1. The U.S. government is a republic and a democracy and is guided by the principle of federalism.
2. Citizens of the U.S. have the right to vote in free elections.
3. The purpose of the system of checks and balances is to make sure none of the three branches of government has too much power.

2 Building background knowledge on the topic Page 4
A

1. T   2. F   3. F   4. T   5. F
6. T   7. F   8. T   9. F   10. F

3 Previewing the topic Page 5
B

a. 3   b. 5   c. 1   d. 4   e. 2

2 Real-Life Voices

Before the Interviews

1 Building background knowledge and vocabulary Pages 6–7
A

1. b   2. c   3. g   4. d
5. e   6. f   7. a

B

1. elections
2. going to the polls
3. compulsory
4. candidate
5. party
6. issue
7. run for office

2 Examining graphics Page 7

1. It shows all of these: facts (percentages of the population who voted); a trend (that voting percentages have remained fairly consistent); and comparisons (e.g., a higher percentage voted in 1960 than in 1980).
2. 1940 and 1960
3. There was a decrease in the percentage of voters.
4. About 58%
5. Student answers will vary.

Interview 1 – Reasons for Voting or Not Voting

2 Listening for different ways of saying *yes* and *no* Page 8
A

1. b   2. a   3. d   4. c

3 Listening for tone of voice Page 9

1. unsure
2. certain
3. excited
4. hopeless

Interview 2 – Voter Turnout

2 Listening for main ideas Page 10
B

1. a   2. c   3. b   4. c, d

4 Academic Listening and Note Taking

Before the Lecture

1 Listening for the plan of a lecture Page 14
A

1. c   2. a   3. b   4. d   5. e

B

Order: 3, 1, 4, 5, 2

Lecture Part 1 – The Three Branches of the U.S. Federal Government

1 Guessing vocabulary from context Page 16

B

a. 2   b. 5   c. 8   d. 4
e. 3   f. 1   g. 6   h. 7

2 Using information the lecturer puts on the board Page 17

A

Branch of government	Legislative	Executive	Judicial
Name	Congress: – Senate – House of Representatives	*president*	*Supreme Court*
Name of officials	senators representatives	*president vice president secretaries*	*justices*
Responsibility	makes laws	*approves laws*	*interprets laws*
Details	Senate = 100 members (2 from each state) House = 435 members *(number depends on size of state population)*	*many secretaries: – Secretary of State – Secretary of Defense – Secretary of Education etc.*	*– 9 justices – decide if laws are constitutional*

Lecture Part 2 – The System of Checks and Balances

1 Guessing vocabulary from context Page 17

B

1. a   2. d   3. e   4. c   5. b

2 Taking good lecture notes Page 18

B

The System of Checks and Balances

Why is fed. gov. divided
into branches? } wrote main ideas
    Founders wanted to avoid
    dictatorship
    Invented system of checks
    & balances
    3 branches have sep respons + ← wrote only important words instead of complete sentences
    have power to check
    (limit) each other's actions ← used abbreviations and symbols
Ex:
    1. Selection of Supreme Court Justices
       – pres. chooses Justices, but Cong.
         can disapprove } indented examples and details
    2. Cong. passes laws, but pres. can veto
    3. Cong. passes law & pres. signs, but Supreme
       Court can say it's unconstitutional

Chapter 2
Constitutional Issues Today

1 Getting Started

1 Reading and thinking about the topic Page 19
B

1. In 1787, George Washington, James Madison, Alexander Hamilton, and other leaders met in Philadelphia to talk about how to organize the new government of the United States. The result of their work was the U.S. Constitution.
2. The Bill of Rights is the first 10 amendments added to the Constitution in 1791, which include freedom of speech, freedom of religion, and the right of people accused of crimes to have a lawyer.
3. Censorship and whether or not the government can listen to private telephone conversations are two controversial topics.

2 Understanding numbers, dates, and time expressions Pages 20–21
B

July 1, 1971	9. Voting age lowered from 21 to 18
1920	8. Women win right to vote
from 1787 to 1920	7. Only men had right to vote
1870	6. African American men win right to vote
1865	5. Slavery ended
from 1861 to 1865	4. American Civil War
1791	3. Bill of Rights became part of U.S. Constitution
1789	2. Constitution adopted
July 4, 1776	1. United States declared independence from Britain

2 Real-Life Voices

Before the Interviews

2 Previewing the topic Page 22
B

a. First
b. Sixth
c. Second
d. Fourth
e. First
f. First
g. First
h. Fifth
i. First

Interview 1 – Important Constitutional Rights

2 Listening for specific information Page 24
B

1. b   2. a   3. a   4. a
5. a   6. a   7. a   8. b

Interview 2 – A Controversial Right

2 Listening for specific information Page 25
B

1. bear arms
2. Second
3. two
4. criminals
5. legal
6. responsible
7. good
8. sports
9. self-protection
10. police
11. need

3 Listening for stressed words Page 26

1. b, d   2. b, c   3. b, d

4 Academic Listening and Note Taking

Before the Lecture

2 Listening for main ideas and details Page 31
A

Excerpt 1:
4
1
6
3
2
5

Excerpt 2:
6
4
1
5
3
2

Lecture Part 1 – Overview of the First Amendment

1 Guessing vocabulary from context Page 32
B

a. 6   b. 3   c. 4   d. 5   e. 7
f. 2   g. 9   h. 10   i. 1   j. 8

2 Using symbols and abbreviations Pages 33–34
C

1st amend = 5 f'doms

1. F'dom of relig
    = Am's can practice their relig w/o interference from gov't
    U.S. has no national relig

2. F'dom of spch
    = f'dm to talk openly about ideas
    Inc. "symbolic speech" like clothes
    +/& all forms of exp , meaning words, pictures

3. F'dom of the press
    = f'dom to publish diff ideas & opinions
    Inc. books, newspapers, magazines, and Internet arts .
    cartoon making joke about pres is legal
    journalist can write article criticizing the gov't

4. F'dom of assembly
    = can meet in grps
    Sts can participate in college demonstration

5. F'dom of petition
    = citizens have f'dom to ask gov't to change things

    To sum: we use the term f'dom of exp to talk about all 5 f'doms .

Lecture Part 2 – First Amendment Controversies

1 Guessing vocabulary from context Page 34

B

1. c   2. d   3. e
4. a   5. b   6. f

2 Using a map to organize your notes Page 35

C

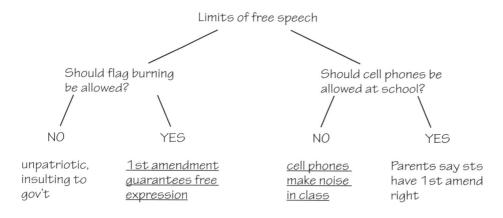

Limits of free speech

Should flag burning be allowed?

NO — unpatriotic, insulting to gov't

YES — 1st amendment guarantees free expression

Should cell phones be allowed at school?

NO — cell phones make noise in class

YES — Parents say sts have 1st amend right

What does f'dom of relig mean in practice?

e.g. Allow children to pray in pub. schools?

YES
1st amend guar. f'dom of relig.

NO
1st amend also says no nat'l relig.
Schools = public, so no relig. activity allowed

Courts say: Private prayer OK, but if org'd by school – no

Unit 1 Academic Vocabulary Review

A Page 37

1. demonstration
2. environmental
3. challenge
4. authorized
5. inconclusive
6. controversial
7. founding
8. interpret
9. identification
10. illegal
11. symbolizes
12. requirement
13. participate
14. obviously
15. similarly

Chapter 3
The Origins of Diversity

1 Getting Started

1 Reading and thinking about the topic Page 44
B

1. The United States is considered a county of immigrants because its people come from a variety of religious, economic, racial, and ethnic backgrounds.
2. The largest groups to come to the U.S. at this time were the Germans, Irish, Italians, and Jews. Some came for better economic opportunities, and others came for political and religious freedom.

3 Listening for numerical information Page 45
B

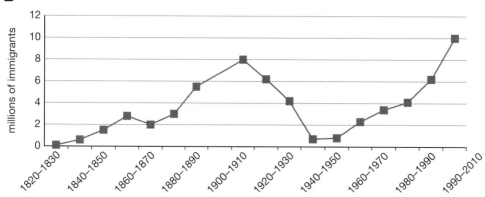

2 Real-Life Voices

Before the Interviews

1 Building background knowledge on the topic Page 46
A

"Push" factors:

a. 4   b. 1   c. 2   d. 3

"Pull" factors:

a. 3   b. 1   c. 4   d. 2

B
1. Pull a
2. Push c
3. Pull d
4. Push a
5. Push a
6. Pull b
7. Push b

2 Examining graphics Page 47
B

1. northern and western Europe
2. 1880–1900
3. rose a little
4. stayed about the same

Interview 1 – Immigration to the United States in the 1860s

2 Answering true/false questions Page 48
B

1. F They met in Ireland.
2. F They came for economic reasons.
3. F Everyone in the family came to the U.S.
4. T
5. T
6. T
7. F They were involved in city politics, and worked in factories, construction, the police force, and as firefighters.
8. F He comes from a very large family.

3 Listening for tone of voice Pages 48–49

Excerpt One: c
Excerpt Two: a
Excerpt Three: a

Interview 2 – Immigration to the United States in the 1900s

2 Listening for specific information Page 50
B

	Eunice	John
Ethnic or religious background	*Jewish*	*Italian*
Country their relatives came from	*Russia*	*Italy*
Reasons their relatives came to the United States	*Religious: fear of religious persecution* *Political: couldn't criticize the government* *Economic: chance to have better jobs*	*Economic: the economy was bad, and they couldn't make a living*
Experience of their relatives in America	*Difficult, because they were very poor. It was also hard to keep the family close.*	*The trip was hard, and when they arrived they had no money and didn't speak the language. The Depression was a very hard experience.*

4 Academic Listening and Note Taking

Before the Lecture

1 Taking notes on handouts Page 54
A

UNIT 1: Prejudice Toward Immigrant Groups
Readings:
1. Strong Anti-Irish Sentiment Begins to Grow
2. Widespread Anti-Immigrant Feelings
3. Religious Prejudice and Stereotypes

UNIT 2: Contributions of Immigrant Groups
Readings:
1. Many Unskilled Workers Needed for Nation's Infrastructure
2. Jobs in Construction and Services
3. Needs of Agricultural and Industrial Production

2 Listening for transitional phrases that introduce supporting details Page 55
B

1. for instance
2. in fact
3. One reason for this was
4. in other words

Lecture Part 1 – Immigrants Face Challenges

1 Guessing vocabulary from context Page 56
B

a. 6   b. 5   c. 1
d. 3   e. 2   f. 4

2 Using telegraphic language Page 57
B

Imms Face Prejudice

  I. <u>4 maj imm grps imm'ed to U.S. @ this time</u>:
      Germans, Irish, Jews (eastern Europe), Italians
 II. Prejudice
      Ex: <u>call imms cruel names</u>, refuse to rent them
        apt. or give them jobs
III. <u>Reasons for prej</u>
      A. <u>Size of imm pop</u>: 30 mill
      B. Diff relig
      Ex: <u>prej vs Catholics + Jews</u>
      C. <u>Diff langs +</u> unfamiliar customs, foods,
        clothes, etc.
      D. People scared imms would not share
        democ. values
      Ex: <u>prej vs Germans during WWI</u>
      E. Amers. afraid of losing jobs

Lecture Part 2 – Immigrants Make Contributions

1 Guessing vocabulary from context Page 58
B

1. e   2. b   3. a
4. f   5. c   6. d

2 Organizing your notes in columns Page 59
B

Immigrants Make Lasting Contributions

Immigrant Groups	Examples of Contributions
<u>Germans</u>	<u>farmers</u>, tailors, bakers, butchers
Irish	built <u>infrastructure of many Am cities</u> inc. skilled wkrs, ex: <u>plumbers</u> + unskilled, ex: <u>factory wkrs</u>
<u>Jews</u>	<u>popular music</u>, entertainment, education, science, <u>clothing</u> industry
<u>Italians</u>	built <u>roads</u>, canals, <u>bridges</u>, buildings, and <u>railroads</u>
All imms	contrib to <u>ec</u> and <u>culture</u> ex: <u>langs, food</u>, music, relig, lifestyles

After the Lecture

1 Answering multiple-choice questions Page 60
A

1. a   2. b   3. a
4. b   5. a   6. c

Chapter 4
Diversity in the United States Today

1 Getting Started

1 Reading and thinking about the topic Page 63
B

1. A century ago, most immigrants to the United States came from Europe. Since 1965, they have come from countries such as Mexico, China, and India as well as the Caribbean and eastern Europe.
2. Immigrants continue to come for economic and political reasons and also because of Americans' acceptance of diversity, educational opportunities, and health care.
3. Some come to join their families, while others leave their families behind. Some are poor, and others make a lot of money. Some adapt completely, some maintain a "hyphenated" identity, and some keep their original culture for their whole lives.

2 Listening for percentages and fractions Page 64
B

1. The time periods shown are: 1901–1940, 1941–1980, and 1981–2000.
2. Asia, Europe, and Latin America are all included.
3. Student responses will vary.

C

Chart 1:
Europe: 79%
Latin America: 6%
Asia: 4%
Other: 11%

Chart 2:
Europe: 34%
Latin America: 34%
Asia: 19%
Other: 13%

Chart 3:
Latin America: 47%
Asia: 34%
Europe: 13%
Other: 6%

D

1. The percentage of immigrants from Europe has gone down. The percentage of immigrants from Latin America and Asia has risen.
2. Between 1981 and 2000, 47% (almost 1/2 of all immigrants) came from Latin America, and 34% (about 1/3) came from Asia. Only 13% came from Europe.
3. Student response will vary.

2 Real-Life Voices

Before the Interviews

2 Building background knowledge on the topic Page 65
C

1. b   2. c   3. d   4. e
5. f   6. g   7. a

Interview 1 – Reasons for Coming to the United States

2 Listening for specific information Page 66
B

	Agustín	Nadezhda	Chao
Country of origin	Mexico	Russia	China
Length of time in the U.S.	Over 20 years	6 years	10 years
Reason(s) for coming	Work	Better educational opportunities for her children	To join his family To study
Difficulties in the beginning	Didn't know anyone except for brother Unsatisfying jobs	Hard to leave her country and her mother	Hard to learn English Hard to work and study at same time
Life now	Works in a food store In contact with family back home	Just became a citizen	Loves living in U.S. Studying to make dream come true

Interview 2 – Adapting to Life in the United States

2 Listening for specific information Page 67

B

Mateo

1. the Dominican Republic
2. the States
3. hybrid
4. American
5. Dominican
6. Spanish
7. Latin music
8. Dominican
9. world
10. back and forth

Minsoo

1. Korea
2. Korean
3. work
4. opinion
5. Korean
6. absorbing

Abdoul-Aziz

1. Niger
2. adult
3. English
4. French
5. African
6. his family
7. switching
8. identity
9. mixture

3 Listening for stressed words Page 68

B

Excerpt One: a
Excerpt Two: c
Excerpt Three: b

3 In Your Own Voice

Pages 69–70

A

1. c   2. d   3. e   4. i   5. j
6. a   7. b   8. f   9. g   10. h

C

1. b   2. h   3. c   4. g   5. d
6. i   7. a   8. e   9. f

4 Academic Listening and Note Taking

Before the Lecture

1 Previewing the topic Page 71
A

1. melting pot
2. salad
3. (patchwork) quilt
4. kaleidoscope

2 Listening for definitions Page 72
A

1. metaphor/figure of speech
2. melting pot/metal container
3. salad/dish
4. patchwork quilt/cover for a bed
5. kaleidoscope/tube

Lecture Part 1 – Metaphors for American Society

1 Guessing vocabulary from context Page 73
B

1. h   2. c   3. d   4. e
5. g   6. f   7. b   8. a

2 Reviewing and revising notes Pages 75–76
D

Salad Bowl Metaphor
1. Salad = dish made of different vegetables that are mixed together
2. Metaphor represents America as a diverse culture
3. Made of different races, ethnic groups, cultures, and languages
4. Each group keeps parts of its own culture

Quilt Metaphor
1. Quilt = a cover for a bed that is made from pieces of cloth sewn together
2. Shows that we're all unique but we're all connected

Kaleidoscope Metaphor
1. Kaleidoscope = a kind of tube that you can look through; you turn it to see complex, changing patterns
2. Dynamic metaphor, showing America as a beautiful picture that is always changing

Lecture Part 2 – Transnationalism

1 Guessing vocabulary from context Page 76
B

a. 4   b. 5   c. 1
d. 3   e. 2   f. 6

2 Using bullets to organize your notes Page 77
B

Transnationalism = immigrants maintain relationship with their countries of origin	Examples of transnationalism: • imms may own homes, land or businesses in countries of origin • send money to family members • support sports teams • travel home frequently • get involved in business or political affairs
World is getting smaller and smaller	Ways that immigrants stay connected: • go back and forth often • stay connected by phone or Internet • send money home

Unit 2 Academic Vocabulary Review

A Pages 79–80

a. adapt
b. complexity
c. communicating
d. adaptation
e. diverse
f. diversity
g. cultural
h. contributions
i. ethnic
j. energy
k. energetic
l. economic
m. involving
n. involvement
o. expanded
p. identify
q. unique
r. professional
s. survive
t. uniquely

Chapter 5
The Struggle Begins

1 Getting Started

1 Reading and thinking about the topic Page 86
B

1. The Civil War, the passage of the 13th, 14th, and 15th Amendments, and the 1954 Supreme Court decision all led to greater equality for African Americans.
2. After the passage of the 19th Amendment, women were able to vote. Many women worked outside their homes for the first time during World War II.
3. The Civil Rights Act and Equal Pay Act helped both blacks and women. These acts made it illegal to discriminate against workers because of their race or gender and legalized equal pay for men and women.

2 Building background knowledge on the topic Page 87
A and B

a. 1776
b. 1960s
c. 1920
d. 1954

2 Real-Life Voices

Before the Interviews

1 Building background knowledge on the topic Page 88
A

1. T   2. T   3. F
4. F   5. T   6. T

C

All statements are true.

Interview 1 – A Personal Encounter with Segregation

2 Listening for answers to *Wh-* questions Page 89
B

1. Cynthia was with her parents and brothers and sisters.
2. At a gas station, Cynthia went to drink from a water fountain. The owner grabbed her because the fountain was for whites only.
3. It happened before the civil rights movement.
4. They were going from New York to South Carolina to spend time with family.
5. Cynthia's father couldn't guarantee the family's safety and couldn't protect her.

Interview 2 – An Inspiring Time

2 Listening for specific information Page 91
B

1. c   2. b   3. b   4. c
5. c   6. a   7. b   8. b

3 Listening for stressed words Page 91
B

Excerpt One
1. a   2. d
Excerpt Two
3. b   4. d
Excerpt Three
5. a   6. d

4 Academic Listening and Note Taking

Before the Lecture

1 Building background knowledge on the topic Page 95
B

1. Rosa Parks refused to give up her seat on the bus. She was arrested and lost her job.
2. They did not ride city buses for more than a year.
3. Martin Luther King Jr. supported the boycott, and spent 2 weeks in jail because of it.

2 Listening for guiding questions Page 96
B

1. b   2. a   3. d   4. c

Lecture Part 1 – The Civil Rights Movement

1 Guessing vocabulary from context Page 97
B

1. d   2. f   3. a
4. c   5. b   6. e

2 Creating your own symbols and abbreviations Page 98
C

Pt. 1 The Civil Rts Movt

What was it?	strug. by 100s of 1000s of people to achieve Eq rts for Af Ams
How did it start?	100 yrs. after end of slav., seg + discr still common ⇒ beg. of civ rts movt
Key events:	1. Dec 1, 1955: Rosa Parks refused to give up bus seat ⇒ Montgomery bus boycott
	2. 1960: blk. sts refused to leave a rest = owner wouldn't serve b/c of color ⇒ sit-ins
	3. March 1963: March on Washington 200,000 people heard MLK give "I Have a Dream" speech
What happened next?	More protests, demons, sit-ins – strug to stop prej + discr
Achievements?	1. Jim Crow laws overturned
	2. fed gov't passed laws like Civ Rts Act + Voting Rts Act
	3. ⇒ other gps began fighting for just + equal

Lecture Part 2 – The Women's Movement

1 Guessing vocabulary from context Page 99

B

a. 6   b. 2   c. 4
d. 1   e. 5   f. 3

2 Organizing your notes in a chart Page 100

B

Pt 2: The women's movt			
WWII	**1950s**	**1960s**	**Today**
♂: fighting in Europe, Asia ♀: took over ♂ jobs factories, construction, offices 1945: ♂ came back home → ♀ left jobs	→ ♀ started to feel dissat. w/ roles – 30% worked = earned less than ½ of what ♂ earned for = job – could be teachers, nurses, secs – no ♀ managers	1963: journalist Betty Friedan wrote bk Book showed ♀ unhappy w/ lives → beg. of women's movt Mid 60s: ♀ demanded = opps	Successes of WM: – = pay for = wk – more ♀ than ♂ in college – more control over lives But: - today ♀ make only 80c for $1 ♂ make – 12 weeks out of work for baby Ineq. still exists

Chapter 6
The Struggle Continues

1 Getting Started

1 Reading and thinking about the topic Page 103
B

1. Groups that have struggled for equality since the 1960s include Hispanics, older people, Native Americans, and people with disabilities.
2. The protests of Latinos have led to ethnic studies programs at U.S. colleges. Older Americans are guaranteed more access to public services. Public schools must provide assistance to children with disabilities.
3. Racism, sexism, ageism, and prejudice against people with disabilities still exist. Laws have been passed, but they are not always enforced.

2 Listening for specific information Page 104
B

1. Peter is <u>55</u> years old. <u>Five</u> months ago, he lost his job as a <u>computer programmer</u> because the company didn't have <u>enough work</u> for him. But then the company hired a new <u>programmer</u> who is <u>26</u> years old.
2. Theresa is a <u>journalist</u>. Last week she had an <u>interview</u> for a job with a <u>magazine</u>. It went well until <u>the end</u>, when the interviewer asked her if she was pregnant. She said <u>yes</u>. She didn't get the job.
3. Robert is married and has <u>three</u> children. Last week, he and his wife filled out an application for a new <u>apartment</u>. However, they didn't get it. A friend told them it's because nobody else in the building has <u>children</u>, and the manager is worried about <u>noise</u>.
4. Rebecca is a <u>university student</u> who uses a <u>wheelchair</u>. One of her classes is on the <u>8th</u> floor, and the building only has two <u>elevators</u>, so she has been <u>late</u> to class a few times. She explained the problem to her professor, but he expects her to come to class <u>on time</u> just like everyone else.

2 Real-Life Voices

Before the Interview

1 Thinking critically about the topic Page 106
B

1. Blog 1: African Americans; Blog 2: people whose first language is other than English; Blog 3: people with physical disabilities; Blog 4: young people
2. Blog 1: stereotyping African Americans as poor and violent; Blog 2: employer harassment of immigrants speaking other languages; Blog 3: building access for people with disabilities; Blog 4: store owners suspicions that young people steal things
3. Student responses will vary.

2 Building background knowledge on the topic Page 106
B

1. c	2. b	3. a
4. a	5. b	6. b

Interview 1 – Issues of Inequality

2 Listening for main ideas Page 107
B

	Group	Progress toward equality	Problems that still exist
Jairo	*Latinos*	*– Latinos recog at every level – sports, entertainment, on the job* *– Latinos in gov: mayors, Cong.* *– many services now avail in Span + other langs*	*– poverty in the Hisp comm.* *– access to health care or high quality educ*
Sandy	*Senior citizens*	*– illeg to discr against people because of age* *– hiring and firing*	*– laws hard to enforce*

Interview 2 – Working with the Blind

2 Listening for specific information Page 108
B

a. computer
b. Braille
c. talking clock
d. tray
e. $5 bill

3 Listening for tone of voice Page 109
A

Excerpt One: a
Excerpt Two: a
Excerpt Three: b

4 Academic Listening and Note Taking

Before the Lecture

2 Listening for signal words and phrases Page 115
B

1. To refresh your memory
2. first/third
3. Before
4. In other words
5. In addition,
6. also/because
7. In terms of
8. the most important
9. because

Lecture Part 1 – The Age Discrimination in Employment Act

1 Guessing vocabulary from context Page 116
B

a. 4   b. 7   c. 3   d. 5
e. 6   f. 1   g. 8   h. 2

2 Indenting Page 117
B

Age Discrim. in Employment Act

1. Why law was needed
   – Older people faced discrim. in wkplace
   – Before law, employers could set age limits, ex. 35
2. What the law does
   – Protects people > 40 from discrim.
   – Can't use age to
     • refuse to hire
     • fire
     • promote to a better position
3. Impact of law
   – Nowadays, nothing about age in job app
   – Equal benefits for older + younger people
   – No mandatory retirement
4. Do employers follow law?
   – 1000s of complaints per year – age discrim. still exists
   – Recent study showed companies 40% more likely to interview younger applicant
   – But: People more aware of age discrim. than before law

Lecture Part 2 – The Americans with Disabilities Act

1 Guessing vocabulary from context Page 118

B

1. d   2. c   3. b   4. e
5. g   6. a   7. f

2 Using an outline Page 119

C

The Americans with Disabilities Act (ADA)

I. ADA
  A. Passed in 1990
  B. Protects ppl w/disabil. In diff places, ex:
    1. Work
    2. Housing
    3. Educ.
II. Def. of "disability"
  A. Physical
  B. Mental
III. Impact of ADA
  A. Changed life for disabled people, ex:
    1. Buses have mechanisms to help ppl in wheelchairs
    2. Doorways must be wide
    3. Some businesses hiring ppl w/nonphysical (mental) disab
    4. Sts w/ learning disab can get more time on tests
  B. Most important impact of law: Change ppl's thinking
    1. Some countries: Disabled stay home b/c no way to get around
    2. U.S. Understand there are many things diabled ppl can do
      – Pres. Bush (1990): "Let the shameful wall of exclusion finally come tumbling down."
    3. Goal must be inclusion

Unit 3 Academic Vocabulary Review

A Page 121

I.
1. d   2. c   3. b   4. e   5. a
II.
1. goal
2. promoting
3. impact
4. positive
III.
1. Discrimination
2. create
3. traditions
4. achievement
5. reaction

Chapter 7
American Values from the Past

1 Getting Started

1 Reading and thinking about the topic Page 128
B

1. Values are beliefs that help us decide what is right and wrong and how we should behave. They affect every aspect of our lives.
2. Greek and Roman civilizations and the religious beliefs of Judaism and Christianity, particularly the Protestant tradition, have influenced American values.
3. Some key American values are: hard work, self-reliance, equality, freedom, individualism, justice, and democracy.

2 Listening for specific information Page 128
B

1. Ben
2. have died
3. has few friends
4. positive
5. rich stranger
6. Harvard University
7. good luck and determination

2 Real-Life Voices

Before the Interviews

1 Building background knowledge on the topic Page 130
B

Group A
1. a   2. d   3. b
4. f   5. c   6. e

Group B
1. d   2. f   3. c
4. a   5. b   6. e

Interview 1 – Personal Values

2 Answering true/false questions Pages 132–133
B

Marielena
1. F   2. NI   3. F
4. NI   5. T   6. T

Dan
1. F   2. NI   3. T
4. T   5. NI   6. F

3 Listening for tone of voice Page 133
B

Excerpt One: c
Excerpt Two: a
Excerpt Three: a
Excerpt Four: c

Interview 2 – Values in Theory and in Practice

2 Listening for main ideas Page 134
B

1. a   2. b   3. a   4. b
5. c   6. b   7. a

4 Academic Listening and Note Taking

Before the Lecture

2 Listening for key words Page 138
A

1. folk heroes/folk heroes
2. cowboy/cowboys/cowboy/cowboy
3. entrepreneur/entrepreneurs/entrepreneur
4. superheroes/superheroes

Lecture Part 1 – Cowboys and Entrepreneurs

1 Guessing vocabulary from context

Pages 138–139

B

1. a   2. g   3. f   4. d
5. c   6. e   7. b

2 Clarifying your notes   Page 140

B

Intro
Topic: 3 folk heroes = people or ????   *imaginary figures*
Do extraord. things or have   *extraordinary*
  extraord. powers
3 famous ones = cowboy, ??? + superhero   *entrepreneur*
Rep. our most imp. Values

1. Cowboy
   See everywhere: TV, advert, fashion
   Why so popular?
   150 years ago, people
     moved west to ?   *make their fortune*
   Some started catel (sp?) ranches,   *cattle*
     hired c'boys to help
   C'boy became hero b/c work alone,   *self-reliant =*
     self-relant*   *independent*
   Cowboy rep' values: <u>courage</u>,
     freedom, <u>independence</u>

2. *Entrepreneur*
   = starts company → profit
   = gt. ideas, risks
   = symbol of Am. values
   smart + wk. hard + good ideas → succeed
   pop. Since Horatio Alger stories
   Ex. Bill Gates

3. *Superhero*
   Many kinds: Superman, Batman, Spiderman, etc.
   Fast, powerful, symbols of justice + law
   Defend good, punish bad

Lecture Part 2 – Questions and Answers

1 Guessing vocabulary from context   Page 140

B

a. 3   b. 2   c. 7   d. 1
e. 5   f. 6   g. 4

Chapter 8
American Values Today

1 Getting Started

1 Reading and thinking about the topic Page 144
B

1. The Greatest Generation, Silent Generation, Baby Boomers, Generation X, Generation Y (also called Millennial Generation)
2. They are influenced by world events and technological innovations.
3. Conservatives tend to believe in keeping traditional cultural and religious values and oppose sudden change; liberals tend to favor reform and progress more than tradition.

2 Sharing your knowledge Page 145
A

1.
a. Y   b. X   c. BB
2.
a. BB   b. X   c. Y
3.
a. Y   b. BB   c. X

3 Listening for specific information
Page 146
B

Size of Generation Y: 80 million
Percentage of U.S. population: 20%
Six times as big as: Generation X
Values of Generation Y: diversity, tolerance, speed, change, independence and social responsibility

2 Real-Life Voices

Interview 1 – Differences in Values Between Parents and Children

2 Drawing inferences Pages 148–149
A

1.
a. R   b. C   c. C
d. B   e. R   f. B
2.
a. R   b. C   c. B

B

1. Christine
2. Benjamin's mother
3. Rosiane
4. Christine's mother
5. Benjamin
6. Rosiane's father

3 Listening for stressed words Page 149
A

Excerpt One: a
Excerpt Two: c
Excerpt Three: c

Interview 2 – Values in the Workplace

2 Listening for specific information Page 150
A

1. She is a business professor.
2. "If you had your own business, would you hire you?"
3. Not respecting deadlines is unacceptable because "time is money."
4. She asks students to imagine that they are buying a car. They have paid the deposit, but then they are told that they won't get their car for another week.
5. Cooperation and working as a team. In the workplace, people don't work in isolation.
6. Students should have a professional attitude. They should dress, speak, and write in an appropriate way, using a formal tone when speaking and writing.

4 Academic Listening and Note Taking

Before the Lecture

2 Listening for general statements Pages 155–156

B

1. generally
2. usually
3. Most
4. Generally
5. typically
6. But in general

Lecture Part 1 – Conservative and Liberal Values

1 Guessing vocabulary from context Page 156

B

1. e   2. a   3. f   4. b
5. d   6. g   7. c

2 Taking notes in a point-by-point format Page 157

B

Conserv./Lib. Values

1. Role of gov't	Conserv: Not gov't resp. to pay for social progs.
	Lib: Gov't should fix soc. prob's like poverty + illness
2. <u>Taxes</u>	<u>Conserv: Gov't is too big + expen. High taxes unpop.</u>
	<u>Lib: Taxes nec. to support soc. progs.</u>
3. <u>Business</u>	<u>Conserv: Gov't shouldn't interfere w/biz: econ. w/o gov't control can grow</u>
	<u>Lib: Gov't should control + reg. biz</u>
	<u>Ex: If not reg'd, entreprs won't care about wkrs or custs or envir., only profit</u>

Lecture Part 2 – Values and Political Parties

1 Guessing vocabulary from context Page 158

B

1. b   2. a   3. c   4. h
5. g   6. e   7. f   8. d

2 Using information on the board to help you take notes Page 159

B

Values + Pol. Parties

I. Intro
   A. U.S. has 2-party system
   B. In gen: Repub = conserv
         Dem = lib
   C. But ideas change over time

II. Election results
   A. 1964: <u>Maj. voted for Johnson</u>
   B. 1980: <u>>50% of votes went to Reagan</u>
   C. 2000: ½ Bush ½ Gore
   D. 2008: <u>Dem. Party won w/53%</u>

III. <u>Reasons for changes</u>
   A. <u>Econ. Conditions</u>
   B. <u>Internat'l concerns</u>

IV. Conclusion: <u>Ppl not strict conserv. or lib</u>.

Unit 4 Academic Vocabulary Review

A Pages 161–162

1. A   2. N/V   3. A   4. V   5. A
6. V   7. O   8. N   9. O   10. N
11. A   12. V   13. V   14. A   15. N

B

1. At work
   1. constantly
   2. cooperation
   3. team
   4. individually
   5. eventually
2. At school
   1. comment
   2. appropriate
   3. respond
   4. generational
   5. incidentally
3. On the street
   1. dramatic
   2. specific
   3. publication
   4. emphasis
   5. minimum

Chapter 1 • Lecture Quiz

Answer the following questions on Parts 1 and 2 of the Chapter 1 Lecture, "The Structure of the U.S. Federal Government." Use only your lecture notes to help you. Answer each question as fully as possible. You will receive 20 points for each complete and correct answer.

1. Explain the function of each branch of the U.S. government. (**20 points**)

2. What are the two parts of the legislative branch? Who are the people that form this branch? (**20 points**)

3. Who are the most important members of the executive branch of government? (**20 points**)

4. Explain the judicial branch. (**20 points**)

5. Explain the purpose of the system of checks and balances, and give an example of how it works. (**20 points**)

Name: _____

Date: _____

Chapter 2 • Lecture Quiz

Answer the following questions on Parts 1 and 2 of the Chapter 2 Lecture, "The First Amendment." Use only your lecture notes to help you. Answer each question as fully as possible. You will receive 20 points for each complete and correct answer.

1. Explain what freedom of religion means to Americans. (**20 points**)

2. What does the principle of freedom of speech mean in practice? (**20 points**)

3. Give two examples of freedom of the press. (**20 points**)

4. What two other forms of freedom are guaranteed under the First Amendment? (**20 points**)

5. Give three examples of controversies under the First Amendment. (**20 points**)

Chapter 3 • Lecture Quiz

Answer the following questions on Parts 1 and 2 of the Chapter 3 lecture, "Immigrants to America: Challenges and Contributions." Use only your lecture notes to help you. Answer each question as fully as possible. You will receive 20 points for each complete and correct answer.

1. What were some of the major groups that immigrated to the United States from about 1840 to 1917? **(20 points)**

2. In what ways did these immigrants face prejudice? **(20 points)**

3. What were some of the reasons for the prejudice these immigrant groups faced? **(20 points)**

4. The United States needed a lot of workers at this time in its history. Why? **(20 points)**

5. What are some of the contributions that these immigrant groups made to the United States? **(20 points)**

Name: _____

Date: _____

Chapter 4 • Lecture Quiz

Answer the following questions on Parts 1 and 2 of the Chapter 4 lecture, "Recent Immigrants and Today's United States." Use only your lecture notes to help you. Answer each question as fully as possible. You will receive 20 points for each complete and correct answer.

1. What is a metaphor, and why do historians and writers use metaphors to describe American culture and society? **(20 points)**

2. What is the oldest metaphor that the lecturer mentions? What is the problem with this metaphor? **(20 points)**

3. What other metaphors does the lecturer discuss? Which is her favorite metaphor, and why? **(20 points)**

4. Explain the meaning of *transnationalism* and give examples of this phenomenon. **(20 points)**

5. What are some factors that help today's immigrants keep a closer relationship with their home countries? **(20 points)**

Chapter 5 • Lecture Quiz

Answer the following questions on Parts 1 and 2 of the Chapter 5 lecture, "The Civil Rights Movement and the Women's Movement." Use only your lecture notes to help you. Answer each question as fully as possible. You will receive 20 points for each complete and correct answer.

1. Why was the decade of the '60s so important? **(20 points)**

2. What was the civil rights movement, and how did it begin? **(20 points)**

3. What were some achievements of the civil rights movement? **(20 points)**

4. What was the experience of many women during World War II, and what effect did that experience have? **(20 points)**

5. Describe women's protests in the mid-1960s and explain their successes. **(20 points)**

Name: _____

Date: _____

Chapter 6 • Lecture Quiz

Answer the following questions on Parts 1 and 2 of the Chapter 6 lecture, "Two Important Laws in the Struggle for Equality." Use only your lecture notes to help you. Answer each question as fully as possible. You will receive 20 points for each complete and correct answer.

1. Why did the United States need the Age Discrimination Act? **(20 points)**

2. What does the Age Discrimination Act do, and is this law effective? **(20 points)**

3. What is the Americans with Disabilities Act, and when was it passed? **(20 points)**

4. Give some examples of the impact of the Americans with Disabilities Act. **(20 points)**

5. Explain President George H. W. Bush's comment, "Let the shameful wall of exclusion come tumbling down." **(20 points)**

Chapter 7 • Lecture Quiz

Answer the following questions on Parts 1 and 2 of the Chapter 7 lecture, "Three American Folk Heroes." Use only your lecture notes to help you. Answer each question as fully as possible. You will receive 20 points for each complete and correct answer.

1. Why does the lecturer discuss the cowboy, the entrepreneur, and the superhero? **(20 points)**

2. Why is the cowboy such a popular image in U.S. culture? How does the lecturer illustrate the cowboy's attraction? **(20 points)**

3. What values does the entrepreneur represent? Give some examples of entrepreneurs. **(20 points)**

4. When did the superhero image become popular, and what values do superheroes represent? **(20 points)**

5. Explain the lecturer's response to the question about women folk heroes. **(20 points)**

Name: _____

Date: _____

Chapter 8 • Lecture Quiz

Answer the following questions on Parts 1 and 2 of the Chapter 8 lecture, "Conservative and Liberal Values in American Politics." Use only your lecture notes to help you. Answer each question as fully as possible. You will receive 20 points for each complete and correct answer.

1. Why does the lecturer emphasize the fact that we must discuss conservative and liberal values in a general way? (**20 points**)

2. How do conservatives and liberals generally see the role of the government? (**20 points**)

3. How do conservatives and liberals often disagree about taxes? (**20 points**)

4. Describe conservative and liberal views on business. (**20 points**)

5. Why do voting patterns often change so dramatically? (**20 points**)

Photocopiable   © Cambridge University Press 2013

Lecture Quiz Answer Keys

Chapter 1

1. The legislative branch (Congress) makes the laws. The executive branch approves the laws that Congress makes. The judicial branch interprets the laws that Congress passes. In other words, its members decide if a law is constitutional or not.
2. The two parts of the legislative branch are the Senate and the House of Representatives. There are two senators from each state, for a total of 100 senators. The number of representatives from each state depends on the size of the state's population.
3. The most important members are the president, the vice president, and the heads of government departments, who are called secretaries (Secretary of State, Secretary of Defense, Secretary of Education, and so on).
4. The judicial branch of the federal government is the Supreme Court, which is the highest court in the land. It has nine members, called justices. These justices decide whether laws or other courts' decisions are constitutional.
5. The system of checks and balances ensures that no one person or branch of the government has too much power. The three branches have the power to check, or limit, each other's actions. One example is although the Supreme Court justices are chosen by the president, the Senate has the power to approve or deny the president's choice.

Chapter 2

1. Freedom of religion means that Americans are free to practice their religion without interference from the government. There is no national religion.
2. In practice, freedom of speech means being able to talk openly about your ideas, even if other people disagree with them. Americans also have the freedom to read or listen to others' ideas. Freedom of speech also includes "symbolic" speech, including pictures, music, and fashion.
3. The press can criticize the government and even make fun of government leaders. Journalists have the right to oppose the government's actions in print.
4. The other two forms of freedom are freedom of assembly, which is the right to meet in groups, and freedom of petition, which means citizens have the right to ask the government to change laws and policies.
5. Flag burning, cell phones in school, and prayers in public school are three examples of controversies under the First Amendment.

Chapter 3

1. The major immigrant groups were the Germans, Irish, Jews from Eastern Europe, and Italians, as well as people from Greece, Hungary, China, and Mexico.
2. These immigrant groups were refused apartments, refused jobs, and called cruel names.
3. Many Americans were frightened about the size and diversity of the new foreign population. Immigrants also faced prejudice because of their different religious beliefs, languages, and customs. Americans were afraid that they did not share the country's democratic values. Some people were also afraid that they would lose their jobs as a result of immigrant labor.
4. The United States needed a lot of workers because it was a time of great expansion. Cities and industries were growing, and a lot of people were moving west.
5. These immigrant groups became farmers, tailors, bakers, and butchers. They helped build the infrastructure of many American cities. They were also active in culture and education.

Chapter 4

1. A metaphor is like an image or model that is used to help us understand things that are complex, like America's diverse and complex society and culture.
2. The oldest metaphor the lecturer mentions is the melting pot. The problem with this metaphor is that it doesn't always describe today's reality, in which many immigrants do not assimilate into mainstream society.
3. Other metaphors are the salad bowl, the patchwork quilt, and the kaleidoscope. The lecturer's favorite metaphor is the kaleidoscope, which shows America as a colorful picture of a multiracial, multiethnic, multicultural society that is always changing.
4. *Transnationalism* describes a person's experience across nations or cultures or their continuing relationship with their home countries. For example, many immigrants own homes or businesses in their country of origin, send money to family members in their home country, or stay involved in business or political affairs there.
5. Ease of travel and technology are two factors that help today's immigrants keep a closer relationship with their home countries than immigrants in the past could.

Chapter 5

1. The '60s was a time of great and often violent change in the United States. During this decade, there were many political and social movements, such as the movement against the war in Vietnam, the civil rights movement, and the women's movement.
2. The civil rights movement was the struggle by hundreds of thousands of people working to achieve equal rights for African Americans. It started because almost 100 years after the end of slavery in the United States, segregation and discrimination against blacks was still common.
3. As a result of the civil rights movement, the Jim Crow laws were overturned, and the federal government passed laws that guaranteed the rights of black Americans. Other groups also started fighting for justice and equality.
4. During World War II, many women took over men's jobs while the men were fighting in Europe and Asia. When the men returned from the war to their jobs, women felt dissatisfied with returning to their roles as wives and mothers.
5. In the mid-1960s, women marched in the streets, tried to elect more women to Congress, and demanded equal opportunities for women in education and at work. Today, "equal pay for equal work" is the law. More women than men go to college, and there are women politicians and university presidents.

Chapter 6

1. Before the Age Discrimination Act was passed, older people faced a lot of discrimination in the workplace. For example, employers could set an age limit for job applicants.
2. The Act protects people over 40 years old from discrimination at work in areas such as hiring and firing, benefits, and retirement. However, there are still many legal complaints about age discrimination.
3. The Americans with Disabilities Act was passed in 1990 to protect people with disabilities from discrimination.
4. The Americans with Disabilities Act has improved life for thousands of disabled people in the areas of public transportation, access to buildings and other public spaces, and hiring and education practices.
5. This comment means that our goal should be inclusion, meaning equality and full participation in society for all people.

Chapter 7

1. The cowboy, the entrepreneur, and the superhero are images that most Americans know about from traditional songs, stories, or actual history. These images surround us in advertising and daily culture.
2. The cowboy represents courage, freedom, and independence. This image became popular in the nineteenth century when people moved west to make their fortune. The lecturer says the cowboy represents some core American values. He points out that most students wear jeans.
3. The entrepreneur represents the idea that if you are smart, have good ideas, and work hard, you can succeed. Examples include Andrew Carnegie, who made millions of dollars from steel factories, and John D. Rockefeller, who made his fortune in oil.
4. The superhero became popular in the 1930s. Superheroes are symbols of justice and law.
5. The lecturer says most traditional folk heroes were men but mentions Annie Oakley and Wonder Woman as examples of real and imaginary women folk heroes. He believes that there will be more women folk heroes in the future.

Chapter 8

1. The lecturer points out that it is hard to make specific statements about Americans' political views because of the size and diversity of the population.
2. Conservatives tend to put more emphasis on personal responsibility than on government responsibility for social programs. Liberals believe in greater government responsibility.
3. Conservatives usually think government is too big and expensive, requiring higher taxes, whereas liberals tend to think taxes are necessary to support social programs.
4. Conservatives typically support an economy without government control, whereas liberals think business should be closely regulated.
5. Changes in voting patterns can be the result of satisfaction or dissatisfaction with economic conditions or the international situation, or the result of differences in attitude between different generations of voters.

Audio Script

Unit 1: Laws of the Land
CD1 TR02 ## Chapter 1: The Foundations of Government

Getting Started:

Previewing the topic, page 5

Man: Hey, did you ever take a close look at the back of a one-dollar bill?

Woman: No, not really. Is there something special about it?

Man: Well, yeah. See, it has some really interesting symbols on it.

Woman: Let me see. Hmm . . . The two circles . . . aren't they the two sides of the Great Seal?

Man: That's right. And see the pyramid in the circle on the left? It means that America has a strong foundation. And look on the bottom. You see the number 1776 in Roman numerals? That's the year the United States became an independent country. And there are some symbols in the other circle, too.

Woman: Let me get a closer look. There's a bird . . .

Man: Yeah, that's the bald eagle. It's the national symbol of the United States.

Woman: And some writing in Latin . . .

Man: Uh-huh, *e pluribus unum*. That means "Out of many, one." It means that the United States is made up of many states and many people, but it's still one nation, see?

Woman: Yeah, sure. What about the stars above the eagle's head? What do they mean?

Man: They're symbols for the original 13 states. And see, there are other groups of 13 in the Great Seal, too. Like, the pyramid has 13 steps.

Woman: Wow. I had no idea a one-dollar bill was so full of meaning.

Man: I know. It's really interesting. Now I'm going to try to find out what some of the other symbols mean.

Interview 1: Reasons for Voting or Not Voting
CD1 TR03 ### Listening for different ways of saying *yes* and *no*, page 8

Interviewer: I'd like to ask all of you some questions about voting. Manuel, you first: Do you vote?

Manuel: Well, not usually. I mean, I know it's important, but I'm always too busy on Election Day. I can never seem to get to the polls.

Interviewer: Why is that? The polls are open from six in the morning until nine at night.

Manuel: Yes, but it's still not convenient for a lot of people. I didn't vote for president while I was in college because I had too much to do. Then the next election, I had a really crazy day and I just couldn't make it. I don't really understand how in this great democracy people have to work on Election Day. I think we should get a national holiday, like they do in a lot of other countries, so that we can vote.

Interviewer: A national holiday for voting? That's an interesting suggestion. Now what about you, Mary, do you vote?

Mary: Sure. I think it's really important for citizens to vote. You know, voting gives you a voice, a feeling that you have the power to make a difference. When you vote, you get to say who you feel is the best candidate, who can help more in dealing with the country's problems.

Interviewer: And do you believe your vote can really make a difference?

Mary: Absolutely! I mean, if millions of people vote for what they believe, they have a lot of power! I disagree with Manuel. If people really want to vote, they can find time on Election Day to do it.

Interviewer: Kelly, what about you? Do you agree with Mary that voting is important?

Kelly: Yeah, I do. Frankly, I can't understand people who don't bother to vote. I think voting is a civic duty and it should be compulsory. That's what happens in other countries around the world. I read that in 34 countries voting is an obligation. It's required by law.

Interviewer: So do you vote yourself?

Kelly: Of course I do! I voted as soon as I turned 18. And lots of people feel the same way as I do. Take a look at the last election — young people are coming out to vote, and that is making all the difference.

Interviewer: And you, Ralph, do you vote?

Ralph: Nah, I haven't recently. What's the point? I feel like even if I do vote, nothing ever changes. It doesn't seem to make any difference who's in power. Actually, I don't trust most politicians. When they run for office, they make a lot of promises, but then they don't keep any of them.

Listening for tone of voice, page 9
CD1 TR04 ### Excerpt 1 [*sounds unsure*]

Manuel: Well, not usually. I mean, I know it's important, but I'm always too busy on Election Day. I can never seem to get to the polls.

Excerpt 2 [*sounds certain*]

Mary: Sure. I think it's really important for citizens to vote. You know, voting gives you a voice, a feeling that you have the power to make a difference.

Excerpt 3 [*sounds excited*]

Kelly: Of course I do! I voted as soon as I turned 18. And lots of people feel the same way as I do.

Excerpt 4 [*sounds hopeless*]

Ralph: Nah, I haven't recently. What's the point?

Interview 2: Voter Turnout
CD1 TR05 **Listening for main ideas,** page 10

Interviewer: Hi, Robert. Do you think that voting is important?

Robert: Yes, I do, and I think voting is becoming increasingly important. You notice in the news that more and more people are voting these days, especially young people.

Interviewer: Why do you think more people are voting nowadays?

Robert: Well, I think it's because people are more aware of the issues today. Let's face it, there are many problems that need to be addressed.

Interviewer: What problems are people concerned about?

Robert: Well, they're worried about things that affect them personally. And they're also concerned about world events.

Interviewer: What's the most important issue, in your opinion?

Robert: Well, the environment is definitely a critical topic. Scientists have proved that global warming is a huge problem, and we can't go on ignoring it. Already, we see that sea levels are rising. And the problem is just going to get worse unless we take decisive steps to address it.

Interviewer: Are there any other issues that concern you?

Robert; Well, the economy, for one. The government needs to do something about all the people that are out of work. I mean, I understand there's a global economic crisis, but surely we have to make it a priority to get people back to work. So for me, that's the number one issue. And then there's the issue of health care.

Interviewer: Health care?

Robert: Yes. Health care is a big problem, because it's so expensive to see a doctor or get an operation. But I think it's a basic right of every citizen to have adequate medical coverage.

Interviewer: How is voting going to help resolve these issues?

Robert: Well, the political parties are sharply divided over these issues, and if we vote for the representatives we agree with, we can put them in power.

Lecture: Nelson Rodgers, "The Structure of the U.S. Federal Government"
CD1 TR06 **Before the Lecture: Listening for the plan of a lecture,** page 14

Hi. Welcome to you all. My name is Nelson Rodgers. I'm here to represent Ed Sullivan, who was an elected official in New York State for many years. Before that, he also taught English for about 15 years, and he loves to teach students about the U.S. government. He sends you his greetings.

You know, whenever I speak to students, I always get a lot of questions about the basic structure of the federal government. So what I'm going to do today is give you an overview of how the government is organized, and that way, you can start to understand how it works. First, I'll introduce the three branches of government. Oh, uh, I'll be using this chart here on the board to help you understand. And then, after that, I'll explain the system of checks and balances.

Lecture Part 1: "The Three Branches of the U.S. Federal Government"
CD1 TR07 **Using information the lecturer puts on the board,** page 17

Hi. Welcome to you all. My name is Nelson Rodgers. I'm here to represent Ed Sullivan, who was an elected official in New York State for many years. Before that, he also taught English for about 15 years, and he loves to teach students about the U.S. government. He sends you his greetings.

You know, whenever I speak to students, I always get a lot of questions about the basic structure of the federal government. So what I'm going to do today is give you an overview of how the government is organized, and that way, you can start to understand how it works. First, I'll introduce the three branches of government. Oh, uh, I'll be using this chart here on the board to help you understand. And then, after that, I'll explain the system of checks and balances.

All right, now, as you can see on the board, the U.S. government has three branches, or parts, called the legislative, executive, and judicial. So let me start with the legislative branch, which makes the laws. So here on the left, where it says "Responsibility," I'm writing "makes laws." I'll just fill in this box for you as an example. OK. In the U.S., the legislative branch of government is called Congress. And Congress actually has two parts, or houses: the Senate and the House of Representatives. Members of the Senate are called senators, and members of the House are called representatives. Have you got that? OK.

Good. So now let me give you a few more details about Congress. Each state has two senators, and since there are 50 states, there are exactly 100 senators. On the other hand, the House of Representatives has 435 members. That's because the number of representatives from each state depends on the size of that state's population. Obviously, states with larger populations, like California, have more representatives.

All right. The next branch of government I want to describe is the executive branch, which executes, or approves, the laws that Congress makes. And who has that job? The president. Actually the president has many responsibilities, but the most important one is the power to approve laws. Now besides the president, the executive branch also includes the vice president and the heads of government departments, who are called secretaries — you know, Secretary of State, Secretary of Defense, Secretary of Education, and so on.

Finally there's the judicial branch. Judicial is related to the word *judge*. Now, there are three levels of courts in the United States: city, state, and federal. But when we talk about the judicial branch of the federal government, we're usually talking about the Supreme Court, which is the highest court in the land. The Supreme Court has nine members, called justices, and their job is to interpret the laws passed by Congress, in other words, to decide if a law is constitutional or not.

👥 🔊 Lecture Part 2: "The System of Checks and Balances"

CD1 TR08 **Taking good lecture notes,** page 18

OK. Now why do you think the federal government is divided this way? Well, the founding fathers, meaning the men who wrote the Constitution, wanted to avoid a dictatorship. They didn't want one person or one branch to have too much power, and to make sure this didn't happen, they invented a system of "checks and balances." Checks and balances means that the three branches of government have separate responsibilities, but they also have the power to check, or limit, each other's actions.

Let me give you some examples of how checks and balances work. The way Supreme Court justices are chosen is a good example. Supreme Court justices don't get elected. The president chooses them. But the Senate has the power to approve or disapprove of the president's choice. The Senate, in this case, can check the president's power to choose Supreme Court justices.

Here's another example. Let's suppose Congress passes a law, but the president doesn't want to approve it. If that happens, the Constitution gives the president the power to veto it — in other words, he can decide not to sign it. And according to the Constitution, a law doesn't become a law until the president signs it. So in this case, the president is checking the power of Congress.

Let me give you a third example. Suppose Congress passes a law and the president signs it. Is that the end of

the process? Usually yes, but sometimes no. There are times when people challenge the constitutionality of a law. It can be a private citizen or a corporation or a city government who believes that the law is wrong or unfair because it goes against the Constitution. Most cases like that will be heard in a lower-level court. But the Supreme Court has the final authority to decide if the law — which was passed by Congress and signed by the president, remember — is either constitutional or unconstitutional. So this is an example of the Supreme Court checking and balancing the other two branches.

So I hope now that you have a basic understanding of the three branches of the U.S. government and how these branches control each other through a system of checks and balances.

🔊 Unit 1: Laws of the Land
CD1 TR09 ### Chapter 2: Constitutional Issues Today

Getting Started:

Understanding numbers, dates, and time expressions, page 20

1. The United States declared its independence from Britain on July 4, 1776.
2. The Constitution was adopted in 1789.
3. The Bill of Rights became part of the Constitution in 1791.
4. The American Civil War took place from 1861 to 1865.
5. The Thirteenth Amendment ended slavery in 1865.
6. The Fifteenth Amendment gave African American men the right to vote in 1870.
7. From 1787 to 1920, only men had the right to vote.
8. In 1920, the Nineteenth Amendment gave women the right to vote.
9. On July 1, 1971, the Twenty-sixth Amendment lowered the voting age from 21 to 18.

🔊 Interview 1: Important Constitutional Rights
CD1 TR10 **Listening for specific information,** page 24

Interviewer: Hi, Magda. We're here to discuss constitutional rights. Are there any rights that are especially important to you?

Magda: Yes — freedom of speech. And of course that includes the freedom to express yourself in words or in any other way, even if people don't agree with you.

Interviewer: What's your profession?

Magda: I'm a photographer. And in art, freedom of expression is critical. Art is a powerful way of expressing ideas, and that right must be protected, even if the ideas are controversial. I believe censorship is wrong. I don't think anyone has the right to tell people what they can see.

Interviewer: Does that ever happen?

Magda: Yeah, it happens all the time! For example, the government has always censored violent photographs during wartime. And sometimes works of art or works of literature are banned because someone considers them offensive.

Interviewer: Don't you agree with that?

Magda: No, of course not! Look, even if you personally disagree with the message of a work of literature or a piece of art, you have to allow people the freedom to express themselves. That's our constitutional right!

Interviewer: Well, now let me turn to you, Hang, and ask you the same question: Is there any constitutional right that's especially important for you?

Hang: Well, recently I've really come to value the fact that in the United States, we have freedom of assembly. This includes the right to demonstrate and complain and demand change. The First Amendment gives us that right.

Interviewer: Did something happen to make you start thinking about this?

Hang: Yes, there was a big demonstration at my college. I'm a law student. The students wanted the university to stop buying products from companies that use child labor. See, a lot of university products, like hats and T-shirts, are made in countries that allow children to work in factories.

Interviewer: And what happened after the demonstration?

Hang: Well, the university changed its policy; so you see, our protests were very effective. This shows the importance of the right to meet up and express our ideas.

Interview 2: A Controversial Right
CD1
TR11 **Listening for specific information,** page 25

Interviewer: Gloria, let's turn to you now. Can you identify an important constitutional right?

Gloria: Well, the right to bear arms is important to me. I know this is very controversial, and a lot of people disagree with me, but I believe the Second Amendment gives us that right.

Interviewer: Why do people disagree with you?

Gloria: Well, the words of the Second Amendment aren't exactly **clear**. Some people think it means that only the police or soldiers have the right to have guns. But I don't think that's right.

Interviewer: But if everyone has the right to own a gun, aren't you worried that some people will use them for the wrong reasons?

Gloria: Well, yeah, of course, but . . . look, there are two groups of people who own guns. One is criminals . . . and they will own guns anyway, whether it's legal or not! And the second group is responsible citizens who own guns for good reasons.

Interviewer: What are those reasons?

Gloria: Well, some people have guns for **sports**, like hunting or target shooting, and others have guns for self-protection.

Interviewer: Self-protection? Do you think that's really necessary?

Gloria: Yes! The police can't **always** protect people. They can't be everywhere at once, because that's obviously not possible. So store owners and homeowners in some areas might feel they need a gun to protect themselves. I agree with them.

Listening for stressed words, page 26
CD1
TR12 **Excerpt 1**

Gloria: The words of the Second Amendment aren't exactly **clear**.

Excerpt 2

Gloria: Some people have guns for **sports**.

Excerpt 3

Gloria: The police can't **always** protect people.

Lecture: Marcella Bencivenni, "The First Amendment"
CD1
TR13 **Before the Lecture: Listening for main ideas and details,** page 32

Excerpt 1

What does it mean to have freedom of religion? Well, freedom of religion is a very important right. Basically it means two things: First, Americans are free to practice their religion without interference from the government, and second, there is no national religion. Now this freedom affects Americans in many ways. For instance, an employer can't hire you or fire you just because he likes or doesn't like your religion. And freedom of religion includes how you dress. What I mean is, Americans are free to wear any kind of religious clothing they prefer.

Excerpt 2

All right. Now, the next freedom listed in the First Amendment is maybe the most famous one, because it's the one that all of us practice every single day, and that's freedom of speech. What does that mean, exactly? Basically, it means you're free to talk openly about your ideas even if other people disagree with them. You're also free to read or listen to other people's ideas. But in addition, freedom of speech includes what we call "symbolic" speech — like wearing the clothes you like. In fact, the courts have said that freedom of speech includes all forms of expression, meaning words, pictures, music . . . even the way you wear your hair!

Lecture Part 1: "Overview of the First Amendment"

CD1 TR14 **Using symbols and abbreviations,** page 33

Today's lecture is about the First Amendment to the U.S. Constitution, which for many Americans is probably the most important part of the Bill of Rights, because it affects the way we live every day. I'll begin with an overview of the five freedoms in the First Amendment, and after that, in the second part of my talk, I'll tell you about some cases that will show you why the First Amendment is so controversial.

So, now the First Amendment guarantees American citizens five basic freedoms: freedom of religion, speech, press, assembly, and petition. What does it mean to have freedom of religion? Well, freedom of religion is a very important right. Basically it means two things: First, Americans are free to practice their religion without interference from the government, and second, there is no national religion. Now this freedom affects Americans in many ways. For instance, an employer can't hire you or fire you just because he likes or doesn't like your religion. And freedom of religion includes how you dress. What I mean is, Americans are free to wear any kind of religious clothing they prefer. For example, some religions require people to cover their heads all the time, while others require people to take their hats off, for example, in church. Both of these forms of expression are legal.

All right. Now, the next freedom listed in the First Amendment is maybe the most famous one, because it's the one that all of us practice every single day, and that's freedom of speech. What does that mean, exactly? Basically, it means you're free to talk openly about your ideas, even if other people disagree with them. You're also free to read or listen to other people's ideas. But in addition, freedom of speech includes what we call "symbolic" speech — like wearing the clothes you like. In fact, the courts have said that freedom of speech includes all forms of expression, meaning words, pictures, music, even the way you wear your hair!

The third freedom, freedom of press, means the freedom to publish books and articles in newspapers, magazines, and even the Internet. Journalists and publishers have the right to publish different ideas and opinions. Let's say you open a magazine, and you see a cartoon making a joke about the president. You might ask yourself: Is that legal? And the answer is yes. It's also perfectly legal for a journalist to write an article criticizing the government. You can open the newspaper any day and find articles that criticize the government for, oh, let's see, raising taxes or not protecting the environment, or, well of course, military activities in other countries. Journalists are free to agree or disagree

with these actions and express their opinions without fear. The First Amendment lists two other freedoms as well: freedom of assembly and freedom of petition. Freedom of assembly means, very simply, the right to meet in groups. When students participate in demonstrations on college campuses, for example, they are using their right of assembly and the right of free speech at the same time. And the fifth and last freedom is the freedom of petition, which means citizens have the right to ask the government to change laws or change policies. In other words, it means that citizens can complain about the government's actions. I've listed these five freedoms separately, but in real life, we often use the term "freedom of expression" to talk about all of them. Freedom of expression means the right that Americans have to express their views in any form they prefer, for example, by speaking, writing a letter to their senator, demonstrating in the streets, writing a song, or painting a picture.

Lecture Part 2: "First Amendment Controversies"

Using a map to organize your notes, page 35

CD1 TR15 Perhaps you're wondering: Does the First Amendment mean Americans are completely free to say and do whatever they want? And of course the answer is no. There are limits, but trying to decide where and what they are can be very controversial. Let's look at the kinds of questions that our courts deal with all the time.

The first question is: What are the limits of free speech? You see, in practice, there are some restrictions. For example, it's never legal to publish lies about people. But should it be legal to burn the U.S. flag as a form of criticism against the government? Some people say yes because the First Amendment guarantees free expression. But many other people disagree. They think flag burning is unpatriotic and insults the country. You might be surprised to hear that the Supreme Court has ruled that flag burning is legal, but this is very controversial.

Here's another question. Should children be allowed to bring cell phones to school? Many teachers and principals say no, because cell phones make noise in class, and they've tried to forbid cell phones or take them away from children. However, many parents say they need to have a way to get in touch with their children, and they also say that using a cell phone is a form of free speech.

Let's look at another controversial question that often comes up: What does freedom of religion actually mean, in practice? For example, do you think children should have the right to say prayers in public schools? Some people say yes because the First Amendment guarantees freedom of religion, right? But other people say no because the First Amendment also says there cannot be any national religion. And since public schools are open to children of all religions, these people believe there shouldn't be any religious activities in these schools. Basically, the courts have said that students can pray at school privately, but they can't do it during class time, and the school or the teachers cannot organize or encourage any kind of religious activity.

So to conclude what I've been saying, the freedoms promised in the First Amendment can be very controversial. However, freedom of speech is a basic right guaranteed by the Constitution.

Unit 2: A Diverse Nation
CD1
TR16
Chapter 3: The Origins of Diversity

Getting Started:

Listening for numerical information, page 45

Between 1820 and 1830, only about 15,000 immigrants entered the United States. Around 1830, however, immigration to the U.S. began to rise steadily. In spite of a slight dip in the 1860s, immigration continued to climb throughout the rest of the century. The rate fell sharply in the 1890s, but that trend quickly reversed itself.

In the first decade of the twentieth century, immigration figures rose dramatically. From 1900 to 1910, between 8 and 9 million immigrants entered the country, the highest number of immigrants up to that point in U.S. history. Most of these immigrants came to the U.S. through Ellis Island, in New York City.

Immigration began to fall again in the 1910s, however. It continued falling after World War I began in 1914. The number of immigrants dropped even further after the United States entered the war in 1917. New laws were passed in the 1920s that limited immigration, and the Great Depression had begun as well. All of these factors acted to slow down the immigration rate. Only 700,000 immigrants entered the country in the 1930s, and the numbers were even lower in the 1940s.

Immigration increased quickly after World War II. Now, it's climbing rapidly again. Immigration figures today are higher than they've ever been. Over 10 million people entered the U.S. in the first decade of this century.

Interview 1: Immigration to the United States
CD1
TR17
in the 1860s

Answering true/false questions, page 48

Interviewer: Patrick, where did your family come from originally?

Patrick: Ireland. My grandparents both came from the same small village in Ireland. First, my grandfather came over in the 1860s, and then as soon as he got a job, my grandmother came, too. [*excited tone of voice*] You know,

back then, that was the big thing: it was America, America, America! Anyway, after my grandparents immigrated, all the brothers and sisters came, too. And everyone else in the family, too. My father came from a big family — there were ten boys and one girl, and who knows how many cousins.

Interviewer: That's a big family!

Patrick: Yeah. See, the ones in America would send letters back to Ireland. And the letters would say, come on over, there are plenty of jobs over here. You see, over in Ireland, people were desperate. I'm talking about the mid- to late nineteenth century. [*sad tone of voice*] . . and that was the time when, as you probably know, there was a potato famine. That happened in 1848. There was just no food, and people were dying of hunger. It's difficult to imagine this, but about a million people died at that time. But in America, there was opportunity. So the Irish started coming over in massive numbers.

Interviewer: What was life like for them here?

Patrick: Well, they stuck together. The relatives helped the other relatives get jobs. Because one thing that's very important to the Irish is family. They think it's very important to help each other out.

Interviewer: So what happened?

Patrick: Well, what happened was that the new immigrants had to share their apartments, which wasn't always easy. And they didn't have a lot of money. I mean, I think a lot of people arrived with less than $50 in their pockets. So they depended on each other to survive.

Interviewer: Hmm.

Patrick: And then they were Catholic. That set them apart. I've heard there was a lot of prejudice against them because they had different religious beliefs. But on the other hand, they made a lot of contributions to society.

Interviewer: What kind of contributions did they make?

Patrick: [*proud tone of voice*] Well, they got involved in city politics, as voters and elected officials. And they worked hard, in factories for example, and construction work, and in the police force. A lot of them were firefighters. And in these ways they played a very important role in the community.

Listening for tone of voice, page 48
CD1
TR18
Excerpt 1

My grandparents both came from the same small village in Ireland. First, my grandfather came over in the 1860s, and then as soon as he got a job, my grandmother came, too. You know, back then, that was the big thing: it was America, America, America!

Excerpt 2

. . . over in Ireland, people were desperate. I'm talking about the mid- to late nineteenth century . . . and that was the time when, as you probably know, there was a potato famine. That happened in 1848. There was just no food, and people were dying of hunger. It's difficult to imagine this, but about a million people died at that time.

Excerpt 3

They got involved in city politics, as voters and elected officials. And they worked hard, in factories, for example, and construction work, and in the police force. A lot of them were firefighters. And in these ways they played a very important role in the community.

🔊 Interview 2: Immigration to the United States in the 1900s
CD1 TR19

Listening for specific information, page 50

Interviewer: Eunice and John, your families both came to the U.S. in the early 1900s. Could you tell me their stories? Eunice, would you begin?

Eunice: Well, my family is Jewish, and they came from Russia. And for a lot of Jews, you know, there was always a fear of religious persecution. Thousands of Jews were killed in Russia. But in America, there was freedom to practice our religion.

Interviewer: So they came for religious freedom.

Eunice: But it wasn't only for religion, it was political freedom, too. Because in Russia at that time, if you criticized the government, you'd end up in jail! And then the third reason they came here was for the economic opportunities. They wanted the chance to have better jobs and to live more comfortably. They also wanted to make a better life for their children. That's what happened to my grandparents.

Interviewer: So did they have a better life in the United States?

Eunice: Well, they did have more freedom, but they were very poor. My mother used to talk a lot about what it was like when she was a child. You know what the kids got for a gift? An orange! And this was so valued, this piece of fruit. So what I mean is, my family had almost no money at all. But life was difficult in other ways, too. In the United States, it was harder to keep the family close. I think that was probably the hardest thing of all.

Interviewer: And John, what about your family?

John: Well, my family's Italian. My grandparents came from a small village in the south of Italy where my grandfather's family had all been fishermen. Life was very hard for them, too, because the economy was bad, and they couldn't make a living.

Interviewer: What was it like for them to leave Italy?

John: Well, it wasn't easy. The trip alone was a nightmare. I heard a lot of people died on the boat. And when they finally arrived, they were almost penniless, and of course they didn't speak the language.

Interviewer: What happened after they arrived?

John: Let's see, my grandfather got a job in a factory while my grandmother took care of the children and worked part time. They had nine kids! And my father was the youngest one of those nine kids.

Interviewer: That was a big family!

John: Yes, it was. And times were pretty tough because when my parents were born, it was the 1930s, the time of the Depression. But my father was a good student, and he ended up getting a scholarship to college. My father was the first one in his family to graduate from college. That gave him a lot more opportunities.

Interviewer: You sound very proud of him.

John: I am. You know, as I look back on it, I see that my family struggled hard to make a better life in this country. And there was, like, a kind of a feeling of living in two different worlds because they spoke two languages and had two cultures. But they were proud of it, and I am, too.

👥🔊 Lecture: Gerald Meyer, "Immigrants to America: Challenges and Contributions"
CD1 TR20

Before the Lecture: Listening for transitional phrases that introduce supporting details, page 55

1. The four major groups that immigrated to the U.S. during this time were Germans, Irish, Jews from eastern Europe, and Italians. Of course, there were many other immigrants — for instance, from Greece, Hungary, China, and Mexico.

2. Some Americans were worried about the size and diversity of the new foreign population. You have to remember that millions of immigrants arrived during this time, in fact, almost 30 million of them.

3. Most people in the United States were Protestants, and they were often prejudiced against Catholics and also against Jews. One reason for this was that the immigrants' religious practices and traditions seemed strange to them.

4. The Irish, on the other hand, helped build the infrastructure of many American cities — in other words, the canals, the bridges, the railroads, the seaports, and the roads.

👥 Lecture Part 1: "Immigrants Face Challenges"

🔊 Using telegraphic language, page 57
CD1 TR21

Good morning, everyone. Today I want to talk to you about the experience of immigrants who came to the

United States from the middle of the nineteenth to the beginning of the twentieth centuries, from, oh, about 1840 to about 1917. Now as you know, there was some strong prejudice against these early immigrants, but even so, these groups were able to make important and lasting contributions to American society. So, for the next few minutes I'm going to discuss both of these parts of the immigrant experience: the prejudice as well as the contributions.

Now just to remind you, the four major groups that immigrated to the U.S. during this time were Germans, Irish, Jews from eastern Europe, and Italians. Of course, there were many other immigrants — for instance, from Greece, Hungary, China, and Mexico. Many of them met with prejudice in this country. Some Americans called them cruel names or mistreated them. Sometimes they refused to rent apartments to immigrants or give them jobs. So now, what were some of the reasons for this?

Well, to begin with, some Americans were worried about the size and diversity of the new foreign population. You have to remember that millions of immigrants arrived during this time, in fact, almost 30 million of them. And most of them crowded into cities in the eastern and northern parts of the United States. I'm sure it was frightening for many Americans to see so many strangers moving into their cities. But there were other reasons for the prejudice against immigrants, too.

Many immigrants faced prejudice because they had different religious beliefs. Most people in the United States were Protestants, and they were often prejudiced against Catholics and also against Jews. One reason for this was that the immigrants' religious practices and traditions seemed strange to them. Then, third, there was prejudice against new immigrants who spoke different languages and had unfamiliar customs: different foods, different clothes, things like that. Also, many Americans were afraid that the immigrants wouldn't share their democratic values. For example, there was a lot of prejudice against the Germans around the time of the First World War because the United States was fighting against Germany, and people thought Germans living in America might be unpatriotic.

And finally, many Americans were afraid that with all these immigrants coming over, they would lose their jobs . . . that the immigrants would work for less money than they would. And so, for all these reasons, immigrants were seen as a threat to the American way of life.

Lecture Part 2: "Immigrants Make Contributions"

Organizing your notes in columns, page 59

CD1
TR22 What you have to remember is that this time . . . well, it was a time of great expansion in America. Cities and

industries were growing, and a lot of people were moving west, so the country needed a large number of new workers. A lot of these new workers were immigrants who made many important and lasting contributions to the development of the country.

For example, many Germans became farmers. They were good at farming and made important improvements to U.S. farming methods. In addition, Germans also worked as tailors, bakers, and butchers. The Irish, on the other hand, helped build the infrastructure of many American cities — in other words, the canals, the bridges, the railroads, the seaports, and the roads. Many were skilled workers, like plumbers, and others were unskilled factory workers.

Jews — who as I said before, were mostly from eastern Europe at this time — and Italians — also made important contributions to the nation. For example, as the years went by, many Jews became involved in popular music and entertainment. They were also important to the development of American education and sciences. Many also worked in the clothing industry. The Italians, like the Irish, were important in the construction industry and in the building of roads, canals, bridges, buildings, and railroads.

Immigrants brought languages, foods, music, religions, beliefs, and different lifestyles to the U.S. In the end, there's no doubt that they made important contributions to the economy and culture of the United States.

Unit 2: A Diverse Nation

CD1
TR23
Chapter 4: Diversity in the United States of Today

Getting Started:

Listening for percentages and fractions, page 64

Chart 1 shows immigration to the United States between 1901 and 1940. At this time, 79 percent of immigrants came from Europe, 6 percent came from Latin America, and 4 percent came from Asia. Eleven percent came from other places.

Chart 2 shows immigration to the United States between 1941 and 1980. During this period, 34 percent — or about one-third of all immigrants — came from Europe, another 34 percent came from Latin America, and 19 percent came from Asia. Thirteen percent came from other places.

Chart 3 shows immigration to the United States between 1981 and 2000. Forty-seven percent — almost half of all immigrants — came from Latin America, and 34 percent came from Asia. Only 13 percent came from Europe, and 6 percent came from other places.

Interview 1: Reasons for Coming to the United States

CD1 TR24

Listening for specific information, page 66

Interviewer: Agustín, where are you from, and how long have you been in the U.S.?

Agustín: I'm from Mexico. I've been here . . . oh, over 20 years now.

Interviewer: And why did you come?

Agustín: Well, the reason I came, like most Mexicans, I suppose, was to work. In my country there aren't enough jobs. It's hard to make a living.

Interviewer: And what was your biggest difficulty when you came here?

Agustín: The hardest thing for me at first was that I didn't know anyone, except for my brother. I was lucky that he helped me a lot. He sent me money, he gave me a place to live, and he helped me find a job.

Interviewer: And how are you doing now?

Agustín: I'm doing well. When I first came, I was washing dishes, but I didn't want to get stuck doing that. Now I work in a food store, and I work directly with people.

Interviewer: And don't you miss your family in Mexico?

Agustín: Sure, but we're often in contact. I always send money and presents back home.

Interviewer: Nadezhda, what about you? Where were you born, and how long have you been in the U.S.?

Nadezhda: I was born in Russia, and I've been here about six years.

Interviewer: And why did you come?

Nadezhda: Well, mainly because of my children. In the United States, I feel that I can build a better life for them, a rich life with many possibilities.

Interviewer: What kind of possibilities?

Nadezhda: Education. There are more educational opportunities in America. I dream of giving my kids an excellent education. I think that's the most important goal in life.

Interviewer: Was it hard to leave Russia?

Nadezhda: Yes, it was, because I love my country. And, well, my mother is still there, and it was very difficult for me to leave her. But I made a sacrifice for my children. And we are doing well. In fact, I just became a citizen!

Interviewer: Congratulations, Nadezhda! OK, now, Chao . . . you're from . . .

Chao: China.

Interviewer: And how long have you been here, and why did you come?

Chao: I've been here for 10 years. I came for two reasons. The first reason was to join my parents, who were already in the U.S. They left me behind in China with my aunt until they got jobs, but I missed them a lot. And the second reason was to study. I want to become a physician's assistant. It's easier to get that kind of training in the U.S.

Interviewer: Have you had any difficulties?

Chao: Well, it's hard to work and study at the same time. And then it was also difficult to learn English. At home we speak Chinese — only Chinese. And at work — I work in a tofu factory — I only speak Chinese there, too. It's hard, but I love living in America because you can meet people from all over the world and I'm studying to make my dream come true.

Interview 2: Adapting to Life in the United States

CD1 TR25

Listening for specific information, page 67

Interviewer: Mateo, your family is from the Dominican Republic, right?

Mateo: Yeah, my family is, but I grew up in the States. I came here when I was 13.

Interviewer: OK, so, let me ask you: Do you think you're American or Dominican?

Mateo: Let's put it this way: I'm a combination of two cultures. I'm American on the outside, but I'm Dominican inside. That's kind of like being a hybrid.

Interviewer: How do you mean?

Mateo: Well, see, whenever I'm at home, we always speak Spanish because my parents speak very little English. When I go into the house, I feel as if I'm in my home country. I listen to Latin music, I eat Dominican food. . . . You know, it doesn't feel at all American. But whenever I step outside the door, I step into a different world where they speak English and have a completely different culture. So I'm **constantly** going back and forth between the two cultures.

Interviewer: That's a good way to explain it, Mateo, thanks. Now, Minsoo . . . I know you're from Korea, right?

Minsoo: Yes. I've lived here for about five years. I came here because there are a lot more opportunities for **women** here.

Interviewer: Your English is very good. Do you speak it at home?

Minsoo: No, I only speak Korean. It's easier to express myself. I only speak English at work and in college.

Interviewer: Is it difficult for you to speak English?

Minsoo: No, not really. The only time it's hard is when . . . well, in school, for instance, the professor expects us to speak in front of everyone else. I'm not used to giving my opinion in class. In Korea, students are supposed to take notes and do their homework, not talk in class all the time!

Interviewer: Would you say you're more Korean or more American?

Minsoo: I think half and half. 50—50. I have my Korean culture, but I'm absorbing American culture fast.

Interviewer: And Abdoul-Aziz, what about you? You're originally from . . .

Abdoul-Aziz: Niger. That's where I grew up. I came here as an adult.

Interviewer: And you speak . . .

Abdoul-Aziz: Well, it depends on the situation. I speak English at work and school. But I speak French with my friends. And I speak Hausa, an African language, when I call my family back home.

Interviewer: Isn't it hard for you to keep switching languages?

Abdoul-Aziz: Yes, it feels very strange. I feel as if I'm changing my identity every time I switch in and out of English. I keep asking myself: Who am I? Am I Nigerien? Am I American? Or am I a mixture of both?

Interviewer: And does that feeling ever get any easier?

Abdoul-Aziz: Yes, because as my English gets better, I find that I'm changing. I think I'm becoming more and more American these days. My mother says I'm not as **formal** as I used to be.

 Listening for stressed words, page 68

CD1
TR26 **Excerpt 1**

Mateo: So I'm **constantly** going back and forth between the two cultures.

Excerpt 2

Minsoo: I came here because there are a lot more opportunities for **women** here.

Excerpt 3

Abdoul-Aziz: My mother says I'm not as **formal** as I used to be.

Lecture: Betty Jordan, "Recent Immigrants and Today's United States"

CD1
TR27 **Before the Lecture: Listening for definitions,** page 72

1. Metaphors are figures of speech that help us understand complex ideas. They're a kind of comparison.
2. A melting pot is a large metal pot — a kind of container — that's used for melting things, such as different metals or foods.
3. A salad is a dish made up of different vegetables that are mixed together.
4. A patchwork quilt is a cover for a bed that's made from pieces of colorful cloth sewn together.
5. A kaleidoscope is a kind of tube that you look through, and if you turn it, you can see complex, changing patterns.

 ### Lecture Part 1: "Metaphors for American Society"

Reviewing and revising notes, page 76

CD1
TR28 American society today is more diverse and more complex than ever. Over the years, historians and writers have used different metaphors to try to describe this complex American culture. What I'd like to do today is, first, describe four of those metaphors to you, and then, in the second part of the lecture, talk about transnationalism. *Transnationalism* is a word that describes the relationship that recent immigrants continue to have with their home countries.

All right. To begin, let's talk about what a metaphor is. Metaphors are figures of speech that help us understand complex ideas. They're a kind of comparison.

Let's look at our first slide here. This is probably the oldest metaphor for describing American society. It's a melting pot. A *melting pot* is a large metal pot — a kind of container — that's used for melting things, such as different metals or foods. You put different ingredients in the pot, heat them, and the ingredients all melt together and become something new. The picture you're looking at is of a fondue — that's a dish from Switzerland that has cheese and other ingredients — but it's melted, so the original ingredients disappear, and the result is something new and different. This metaphor became popular at the beginning of the twentieth century. And so, according to this metaphor, all immigrants coming into the U.S. would lose their separate identities and assimilate, or mix with the people who were already here, and everybody would come together to create a new and unique culture. You see?

But one problem with this metaphor is that it doesn't always describe reality, especially today's reality, which is that although some immigrants do assimilate, many of them have a different experience. For example, some groups are not accepted by the larger society, or maybe they don't want to mix in completely. So instead, what happens is that many immigrants keep parts of their own cultural identity. For example, they may continue to speak their own language. They may celebrate their own traditional holidays. They usually marry someone from their own race — their own ethnic group. And they might never say they are American, even if they live here most of their lives.

So, if the melting pot isn't a good metaphor for describing American culture, what is? Let's look at the next slide here: a salad in a salad bowl. Of course, a salad is a dish made up of different vegetables that are mixed together, but in a salad, each ingredient keeps its own color and taste. So this metaphor represents America as a diverse culture made of different races, ethnic groups, cultures, and languages that live together, but each group may keep parts of its own culture. Do you understand what I mean? Some people prefer other metaphors for America, like the patchwork quilt. A patchwork quilt is a cover for a bed that's made from pieces of colorful cloth sewn together. Some people like this picture of America because it shows that we're all unique but we're all connected, like the pieces of a quilt. And then a fourth metaphor — you see it here — is a kaleidoscope. A kaleidoscope is a kind of tube that you look through, and if you turn it, you can see complex, changing patterns. This is the metaphor I like best because it's very dynamic. What I mean is that it shows America as a beautiful picture — a multiracial, multiethnic, multicultural society that is always changing.

 Lecture Part 2: "Transnationalism"

🔊 **Using bullets to organize your notes,** page 77

CD1
TR29 So, today's immigrants often keep parts of their own cultural identity at the same time as they become part of mainstream American society.

Today's immigrants also maintain some kind of relationship with their countries of origin — I mean the countries where they or their parents were born. And the word that's used to describe this relationship is *transnationalism*, which comes from *trans*, meaning "across," and *nationalism*, which is of course related to the word *nation*; so a *transnational* is a person whose experience goes across nations or cultures.

Many immigrants own homes, land, or businesses in their country of origin. For instance, I have a student who's building a vacation home in Colombia, even though he lives in New York. Other examples . . . immigrants may send money to family members in their native countries. They might continue to support sports teams there. They may travel home frequently, and they may even get involved in business or political affairs there. My neighbor, who's Japanese, has a business in Tokyo in addition to his business in the U.S. He travels there at least five or six times a year to take care of it.

Now, why do you think immigrants today have a closer relationship with their home countries than immigrants did in the past? Well, there are different factors that make this possible, like ease of travel and new technology. See, travel is now more convenient and less expensive than it was years ago, so people can go back and forth between the U.S. and their homeland more often. Second, communication technology has obviously advanced a lot, too, so it's easy for people to stay in contact by phone or by Internet. It's also easier to send money to other countries. So I hope our discussion has helped you to see that

immigrants today have a complex relationship with their new country America, as well as their countries of origin.

🔊 **Unit 3: The Struggle for Equality**
CD2
TR01 **Chapter 5: The Struggle Begins**

Getting Started:

Building background knowledge on the topic, page 87

a. This is a picture of the Declaration of Independence, adopted on July 4, 1776. It includes the famous phrase "We hold these truths to be self-evident, that all men are created equal."

b. This picture shows an African American man drinking water at a segregated water fountain. Scenes like this were common in the South during the Jim Crow era, which lasted from about 1880 until the 1960s.

c. This picture shows American women demonstrating for the right to vote. Women won this right in 1920, when the U.S. Congress passed the Nineteenth Amendment.

d. This picture shows African Americans protesting school segregation. Legal segregation of public schools ended in 1954 in a Supreme Court case called *Brown versus Board of Education of Topeka*.

 Interview 1: A Personal Encounter
CD2
TR02 **with Segregation**

Listening for answers to *Wh-* questions, page 89

Interviewer: Hi, Cynthia, can you tell me a little bit about yourself?

Cynthia: Well, I'm from New York, but my family's from the South. My parents grew up in South Carolina.

Interviewer: Well, I'd like to ask you about your childhood in the early 1950s. What was it was like before the civil rights movement? What do you remember from that period?

Cynthia: I was a young girl then . . . , and one very clear memory I have is that in August every year, my parents would take us down on a long trip from New York to the South to reconnect with the family down there.

Interviewer: Reconnect?

Cynthia: Yes, to spend the summer together as a family.

Interviewer: How did you get down there?

Cynthia: Well, we traveled by car. So we'd fill the car with pillows for all the children, and we took all kinds of things to eat because we weren't sure you could buy food on the road. You had to plan the food you might need — snacks for the children, sandwiches . . .

Interviewer: Did you know that things were different in the South? Were you aware of segregation?

Cynthia: Well, I'm going to tell you about the moment when I think I really *became* aware. On one of these trips, I remember that we stopped at a gas station, and I jumped out of the car and ran over to get a drink of water from the water fountain. And before I knew it, the owner of the gas station came over and   grabbed me. And he swung me around and pointed to the sign that said "Whites only." And he shouted, "Can't you read?"

Interviewer: You were only a little girl. How did that make you feel?

Cynthia: Well, I remember that I was really startled and obviously scared.

Interviewer: And then what happened?

Cynthia: Well, my father came over, and he seemed really angry, and he told me to get back in the car right away. I ran over and jumped into the back seat, and we drove off. And I kept asking my father why he was so angry. But he wouldn't speak for a long, long time. And then finally, many miles down the road, he stopped the car, and he told us to never, ever leave my mother or him because he couldn't guarantee our safety. And I remember being really confused and upset. No one said anything. It was a terrible experience for all of us.

Interviewer: Oh, I can imagine.

Cynthia: It was just awful. And you know, in recent years, I've tried to talk to my family about that event. My father still doesn't want to talk about it. About how helpless he felt because he couldn't protect his family. But my mother sometimes talks about it. She understands how hard it was for him to be in that position.

Interviewer: That period had a dramatic impact on so many people.

Cynthia: Yes. It's difficult to forget that time. Today, of course, there's been some progress toward equality. After all, in 2008 we elected an African American as President of the United States. And, I am positive and optimistic about the future. But I don't think we can forget the challenges that still exist.

Interview 2: An Inspiring Time

CD2
TR03 **Listening for specific information,** page 91

Interviewer: Hilda, can you talk a little bit about the changes you've seen for women since you were younger?

Hilda: Well, you know, since I was born, there have been incredible changes. It's hard to explain, but life is **very** different for women these days, compared to when I was young, I mean.

Interviewer: Do you mind if I ask how old you are now?

Hilda: No, not at all. I'm in my 70s. And when I went to high school back in the '50s, the typical family was not the same as now. Back then, everyone had a specific role.

Interviewer: A specific role? What do you mean?

Hilda: Well, there was a father who worked outside the house, a mother who was a housewife, and usually two or three children. At least, that was the stereotype. That's what people expected a family to be like.

Interviewer: Did your family fit that description?

Hilda: Yes, it did. My mother stayed home and took care of the children. She did the laundry and the cooking and the shopping. And in fact, all the women in my neighborhood were exactly like my mother. My brother went to college — he was the first one in the family, actually — but there was never any discussion of **me** going to college. Because you know what? Women didn't go to college. They got married and then they had children. You know what people used to say? They said "You don't need a college education to change diapers."

Interviewer: So in other words, they expected you to settle down and get married.

Hilda: Yes. If you were a really successful woman, you could marry a doctor or a lawyer.

Interviewer: Is that what you wanted, too?

Hilda: No, I didn't. I was very ambitious. Do you know what I wanted? I wanted to be a secretary.

Interviewer: A secretary? Not a doctor or a lawyer?

Hilda: No, a secretary! Look, I know that doesn't sound very exciting today, but back then, that was my dream. So I studied typing in high school, and then I graduated and worked as a secretary. I felt as if I was really making progress. Actually, it took a while until I realized that I could do even better than that.

Interviewer: And what happened to make you realize that?

Hilda: Well, in 1965 there was a big women's demonstration in Chicago, where I lived. And I went, and it was phenomenal. The streets were full of women protesting. They wanted to have the same opportunities as men did — to be able to work in any job they wanted to. And you know, those kinds of demands opened my eyes. I thought, I **can** get an education and make something of myself. So after that, I walked into college and registered.

Interviewer: You did? That's great!

Hilda: Yes, and I went to college, and my whole life changed. I became a teacher. Maybe that doesn't seem so exciting either, but back then, it was a big deal.

Interviewer: What do you think of the opportunities young women have today?

Hilda: Today, the situation is so much better. Young girls learn that they can do any job they want. You know, you look around and there are women everywhere. The bus driver can be a woman, or the doctor can be a woman. And women see men in different roles, too. There are men who are nurses and homemakers. When I was young, these were considered women's jobs.

Listening for stressed words, page 91

CD2 TR04

Excerpt 1

Life is **very** different for women these days.

Excerpt 2

There was never any discussion of **me** going to college.

Excerpt 3

I thought, I **can** get an education and make something of myself.

Lecture: Julia Smith, "The Civil Rights Movement and the Women's Movement"

CD2 TR05

Before the Lecture: Listening for guiding questions, page 96

1. So, these are just a few examples of important events in the early struggle for civil rights. What happened next? Well, these events led to more protests, more demonstrations, and more sit-ins throughout the '60s.

2. Today we can look back and be thankful for the great achievements of the civil rights movement. What were some of these achievements? Well, first, the Jim Crow laws were overturned.

3. A journalist named Betty Friedan wrote a book called *The Feminine Mystique*. It was based on interviews with white, middle-class women living in the suburbs. And what do you think Friedan discovered? That these women were very unhappy with their lives because of their lack of freedom and their lack of a sense of identity.

4. Was the women's movement successful? In some ways yes, of course. Today "equal pay for equal work" is the law.

Lecture Part 1: "The Civil Rights Movement"

 Creating your own symbols and abbreviations, page 98

CD2 TR06

The topic of today's lecture is "The Civil Rights Movement and the Women's Movement." Let's see, to begin, let me remind you that the '60s was a time of great and often violent change in the United States. There were many political and social movements. I'm going to be speaking to you about two important movements that not only involved thousands of people all over the nation but also led to new laws that gave us many of the rights we have today.

First, I'm going to talk about the civil rights movement. Do you know about this period in U.S. history? The civil rights movement was the struggle by hundreds of thousands of people working over many years to achieve equal rights for African Americans. You see, almost 100 years after the end of slavery in the United States, segregation and discrimination against blacks was still

common. For example, blacks in many states still couldn't eat in the same places as whites. They couldn't swim in the same swimming pools as whites or sit down on a bus if a white person was standing. The anger that black people felt over these unfair conditions is what started the civil rights movement.

It's difficult to point to the year that the movement began, but there were several key historical events. On December 1, 1955, in the city of Montgomery, Alabama, a black woman named Rosa Parks refused to give up her seat to a white person. This led to the famous Montgomery bus boycott. For one year the entire black community refused to ride on the city buses. The bus company lost a great deal of money, and in the end, the Alabama courts ruled that racial segregation on buses was unconstitutional, and the city of Montgomery was forced to change its policy.

A few years later, in 1960, black students in North Carolina refused to leave a restaurant when the owner wouldn't serve them food because of their color. This kind of protest — they — they were called sit-ins because people would sit and refuse to leave — this kind of protest soon spread like fire all over the South. And how many of you have heard of Martin Luther King Jr.? Well, in 1963, there was a huge national demonstration in Washington, D.C., called the March on Washington, where about 200,000 people heard King give his famous "I have a dream" speech.

So these are just a few examples of important events in the early struggle for civil rights. What happened next? Well, these events led to more protests, more demonstrations, and more sit-ins throughout the '60s, with hundreds of thousands of ordinary people, black and white, struggling together to stop prejudice and discrimination.

Today we can look back and be thankful for the great achievements of the civil rights movement. What were some of these achievements? Well, first, the Jim Crow laws were overturned. This meant that segregation became illegal. Second, the federal government passed laws, like the Civil Rights Act of 1964 and the Voting Rights Act of 1965, which guaranteed the rights of black Americans. Finally, and maybe most important of all, the successes of the civil rights movement led other groups to begin fighting for justice and equality.

Lecture Part 2: "The Women's Movement"

 Organizing your notes in a chart, page 100

CD2 TR07

Now, the women's movement was related in some ways to the civil rights movement, and that's what we'll turn to next. I'm going to tell you about some important events in the history of the movement from the 1940s until today and talk about the movement's main achievements. Now, were you aware that during World War II, when thousands of men were fighting in Europe and Asia, women took over the men's jobs? They worked in factories, in construction, in offices — anywhere they were needed. However, in 1945, when the men returned from the war, the women had to leave many of those jobs and go back home, back to their roles as wives and mothers. But by the 1950s, more and more women were feeling dissatisfied with these roles.

You see, although about 30 percent of women worked outside the home, they were often paid much less, less than half of what men earned, even if they were doing the same job. Plus, women didn't have the same opportunities as men. They could be teachers or nurses or secretaries. The few women working in business had almost no chance to become managers or executives even if they were qualified and worked hard.

Then, in 1963, a journalist named Betty Friedan wrote a book called *The Feminine Mystique*. It was based on interviews with white, middle-class women living in the suburbs, and what do you think Friedan discovered? That these women were very unhappy with their lives because of their lack of freedom and their lack of a sense of identity. This book shocked America. It became a huge best seller, and nowadays, looking back, we can say it marked the beginning of the modern women's movement.

Starting in the mid-1960s, after *The Feminine Mystique* came out, women began to organize and work hard for equal opportunity. They marched in the streets, they tried to elect more women to Congress, they gave speeches, and they wrote letters. They demanded equal opportunities for women in education and at work. They asked, "Why shouldn't women be able to be doctors, lawyers, business professionals, as well as police officers, firefighters, and construction workers?" Of course, these were professions that women didn't traditionally do. But they didn't stop there. Another one of their key demands was "equal pay for equal work."

So looking back, was the women's movement successful? In some ways, yes, of course. Today "equal pay for equal work" is the law. More women than men go to college these days. More students in medical school are women than men. There are women politicians, women on the Supreme Court, and women who are university presidents. It is certainly true that women today have more control over their lives than they did 50 years ago. But we still have work to do. For example, women today still earn only about 80 cents for every dollar that a man earns, and if a woman has a baby, she often risks her job. So we've made great progress, but inequalities still exist.

Getting Started:

Listening for specific information, page 104

1. **Peter:** My name is Peter. I'm 55 years old, and five months ago I lost my job as a computer programmer after working for the same company for 16 years. My boss said the company was losing money and didn't have enough work for me to do. But I heard that they just hired a new programmer who's 26 years old. He's very energetic, but he just doesn't have as much experience as me.

2. **Theresa:** My name is Theresa, and I'm a journalist. Last week, I had a job interview at a magazine. The interview went great until the end, when suddenly the interviewer asked me if I was pregnant. I told him the truth — yes, I am pregnant, but I plan to continue working after my baby is born. But, well, I didn't get the job.

3. **Robert:** My name is Robert. I'm married and I have three children. Last week, my wife and I filled out an application to rent a new apartment. It's close to my work, and a good friend of ours also lives in the building. Our friend told the manager that we are quiet, responsible people, but we didn't get the apartment. Our friend thinks it's because nobody else in the building has children and the manager is worried that our kids will make noise.

4. **Rebecca:** My name is Rebecca. I'm a university student and I use a wheelchair. One of my classes is on the eighth floor, and the building has only two elevators, so I've been late to class a few times. I explained the problem to the professor, but he says it doesn't matter. He expects me to get to class on time — just like everybody else.

Interview 1: Issues of Inequality
CD2
TR09 **Listening for main ideas,** page 107

Interviewer: Hello, Jairo. You're Colombian, right?

Jairo: Yeah. I was born in Colombia, but I moved to the United States many years ago. I'm a college professor.

Interviewer: Is it true that Latinos are the largest minority group in the United States?

Jairo: Yes it is. Hispanics make up something like 16 percent of the U.S. population. It's also the fastest growing minority group, which is why they are an important group to focus on if you are talking about the struggle for equal rights.

Interviewer: What kind of issues do Hispanics confront?

Jairo: Well, the first thing is that they are very important to the country, and that needs to be recognized. As a group, we have made significant contributions to American society. There are Latinos in every sphere of American life: as workers in the economy, and in sports and entertainment, too. And we've made important political contributions. About 300 cities have mayors who are Latinos, and there are more Latino members in Congress than ever before.

Interviewer: Apart from the need for more recognition, what are some other issues that Latinos face?

Jairo: Well, there is a need to provide basic government services in Spanish for non-English speakers. For example, hospitals should have interpreters so that patients don't have to struggle to explain their symptoms in English. And children who don't speak English need to have more help in school. These things are happening to some extent already, but as the Latino population gets bigger, these programs have to be expanded. And by the way, this also applies to people who speak other languages, like Chinese or Russian.

Interviewer: And what about the future? What other progress would you like to see?

Jairo: Well, there's still a lot of poverty in the Hispanic community. Over 25 percent of Latinos still live below the poverty level, compared to only 15 percent for the rest of the population. And poverty creates other problems, of course. Large numbers of Latinos can't get good health care. I hope that will improve in the future.

Interviewer: I hope you're right, Jairo. Thanks. Now, what about you, Sandy? Is there another group you'd like to comment on?

Sandy: Well, if we're talking about the need for more equality, I think we need to talk about senior citizens.

Interviewer: Have they made progress toward greater equality?

Sandy: Well, in some ways they have. Like, since the 1960s, it's been illegal to discriminate against people because of their age. At work, for example, it's illegal to hire or fire someone because they're old.

Interviewer: So that's progress, isn't it?

Sandy: Well, yes and no. What I mean is, there's still discrimination. For instance, my father's in his late 50s now, and recently he lost his job because his company was downsizing. And you know, he's had a lot of trouble finding a new job. I'm sure it's because he's an older worker.

Interviewer: But didn't you just say there was a law protecting the rights of older workers?

Sandy: Well, yes, there are laws, but they're really hard to enforce. A lot of times bosses think there's a risk to hiring older people. Perhaps they think older people might get sick, that's one thing. But older people often get higher salaries because they have more experience. The boss won't say this, so there's no obvious discrimination, but

he'll think it. And if he's got two applicants for a job, and one is older and the other one is younger, he'll hire the younger one. That's what happened to my dad. We still need to work toward changing people's stereotypes about older people.

CD2 TR10

🔊 Interview 2: Working with the Blind

Listening for specific information, page 108

Interviewer: Hi, Robin. I understand you work with the blind.

Robin: Yes, that's right. I work with people who are either partly or completely blind, and basically, I try to help them participate fully and equally in our society, especially at work.

Interviewer: At work?

Robin: Sure, because for example, there are lots of office jobs that blind people can do nowadays, now that there are computers that can "talk" and software that prints documents in Braille.

Interviewer: Really?

Robin: And work is really important. Of course, it gives you a salary, which is obviously one of the main reasons for having a job (laughs). But a job is more than just about money. A job gives you something to do. It gives you an identity, you know, something to talk about and be involved with.

Interviewer: So what exactly do you do?

Robin: Well, I help people who are blind learn the basic skills they need to become independent.

Interviewer: Could you give me some examples?

Robin: Well, think about your day. Think about all the things that you have to do when you get up, go out of the house, and get to work. Now imagine doing all those things without being able to see. The everyday tasks that most people take for granted can be really demanding if you can't see anything. But there are many simple gadgets and techniques that can help blind people function better.

Interviewer: Like what?

Robin: Well, for example, it's useful to have a talking clock. It's just like a regular clock, but it says the time. And there are other items, too, that make life easier, like a tray, which is one of the simplest aids that blind people can use.

Interviewer: A tray? How would they use a tray?

Robin: A tray helps you to keep all your things together. If you put something down on the tray, you know exactly where it is, so you can pick it up again.

Interviewer: Ah, interesting.

Robin: Yes. And then there's money. By folding a bill a certain way, you can tell what kind of bill it is. You leave singles flat. You fold fives from side to side, and tens from top to bottom. You fold twenties both ways. That way, you don't need to rely on other people all the time to help you. Obviously someone has to help you fold the bills once, but after that, you can learn to take care of things on your own.

Interviewer: I would never have thought of that.

Robin: Well, you see, these are simple things that help blind people to live regular lives. Imagine people feeling that their problems are overwhelming, and then they learn how to do things on their own, and it's as if a new world has opened to them. It's very inspiring to watch that process. That's why I love my job.

Listening for tone of voice, page 109

CD2
TR11 **Excerpt 1** [*in an optimistic tone of voice*]

There are lots of office jobs that blind people can do nowadays, now that there are computers that can talk and software that prints documents in Braille.

Excerpt 2 [*in a serious tone of voice*]

Well, think about your day. Think about all the things that you have to do when you get up, go out of the house, and get to work. Now imagine doing all those things without being able to see.

Excerpt 3 [*in an enthusiastic tone of voice*]

Imagine people feeling that their problems are overwhelming, and then they learn how to do things on their own, and it's as if a new world has opened to them. It's very inspiring to watch that process. That's why I love my job.

Lecture: David Chachere, "Two Important Laws in the Struggle for Equality"

CD2
TR12 **Before the Lecture: Listening for signal words and phrases,** page 115

1. Now to refresh your memory, the '60s was an important decade because during this time, several important laws gave more rights to women, African Americans, and immigrants.

2. Let's begin with the first one, the Age Discrimination Act. I think we need to talk about, first, the reasons why this law was needed; second, what it does; and third, well, its impact.

3. Before this law, employers could set an age limit for job applicants.

4. Well, of course, it refers to hiring and firing. In other words, age can't be used as a reason for refusing to hire an older person.

5. In addition, age can't be used as a reason to promote someone to a better position.

6. The ADA also covers people who face discrimination because they have a serious illness.

7. In terms of mental disabilities, there has been progress, too.

8. But I think the most important impact of this law is that it's helped to change the way we think.

9. In many places in the world, people with disabilities have to stay at home because there is no way for them to get around.

Lecture Part 1: "The Age Discrimination in Employment Act"

CD2
TR13 **Indenting,** page 117

Hello, everyone. Now to refresh your memory, the '60s was an important decade because during this time, several important laws gave more rights to women, African Americans, and immigrants. But today I'll talk about two other groups: the elderly — I mean senior citizens — and the disabled. The laws that I'll talk about specifically are the Age Discrimination in Employment Act of 1967 and the Americans with Disabilities Act of 1990.

Let's begin with the first one, the Age Discrimination Act. I think we need to talk about, first, the reasons why this law was needed; second, what it does; and third, well, its impact.

So first of all, why did the United States need this law? Well, the law tried to correct several problems, mainly, that older people faced a lot of discrimination in the workplace. Before this law, employers could set an age limit for job applicants. For example, they might say that only applicants under age 35 could apply.

The law tries to change this situation. Basically, it protects people over 40 years old from discrimination at work and it covers a lot of areas. Well, of course, it refers to hiring and firing. In other words, age can't be used as a reason for refusing to hire an older person, and employers cannot fire older people because of their age, either. In addition, age can't be used as a reason to promote someone to a better position or give them particular jobs.

The impact of this law has been quite significant. If you're applying for a job nowadays, you won't see anything about age on an application. And a second example is that older workers can get the same benefits as younger people — health insurance, and so on. Also, in most cases, mandatory retirement is not allowed nowadays. In other words, your company cannot force you to retire. You might ask: Do employers actually follow this law? Well, there are still many thousands of legal complaints about age discrimination each year, so we have to be realistic about this. There is still some discrimination against older workers. For example, a recent study showed that companies are more than 40 percent more likely to interview a younger job applicant than an older job applicant. However, people are definitely more aware of age discrimination than they were before.

Lecture Part 2: "The Americans with Disabilities Act"

Using an outline, page 119

Now let's turn to the second law — the Americans with Disabilities Act, which is often called the ADA for short. This law was passed in 1990, and it protects people with disabilities against discrimination in different places, for example, at work, in housing, and in education.

By "disability" we mean first, any physical or mental condition that limits a person's ability to participate in a major life activity like walking, seeing, or hearing. The ADA also covers people who face discrimination because they have a serious illness. It covers both physical and mental disabilities.

Let me describe the impact of the ADA. This law has changed life for thousands of disabled people across the country. If you've ridden a public bus in an American city, for example, you know that they all have special mechanisms to help people in wheelchairs get on and off the bus. And doorways have to be wide for the same reason — so that people in wheelchairs can easily get in and out of buildings.

In terms of mental disabilities, there's been progress, too. Today, some businesses are exploring ways to hire people with mental disabilities if they are capable of doing a particular job — like, well, bagging groceries or greeting customers when they go to a store. And students with learning difficulties can get help, such as extra time on tests.

But I think the most important impact of this law is that it's helped to change the way we think. In many places in the world, people with disabilities have to stay at home because there is no way for them to get around, and they are also often rejected by society. We need to understand that having a disability doesn't mean people can't participate in society, and people with particular disabilities can do many things to help them lead happy and productive lives. In 1990, when President George H. W. Bush signed the Americans with Disabilities Act into law, he said, "Let the shameful wall of exclusion finally come tumbling down." In other words, that the wall that had always separated disabled people from everyone else should disappear. Respect is the key here. What this means is that our goal needs to be inclusion — equality and full participation for all people, including people with disabilities.

Unit 4: American Values
Chapter 7: American Values from the Past

Getting Started:

Listening for specific information, page 128

"Wait and Hope," published in 1877, is by Horatio Alger. In the story, Ben's parents have died. Even though he has only a few friends, he refuses to lose hope. In fact, his motto is: Wait and hope. His positive spirit impresses a rich stranger, who gives him a job. Ben is also a very good student and wins an academic competition at school. Because of his good luck and determination, Ben is eventually accepted to Harvard University.

Interview 1: Personal Values

Answering true/false questions, page 133

Interviewer: Marielena, as a mother, what values do you think are particularly important? For example, what values do you try to teach your daughter?

Marielena: Let's see. I've been thinking a lot about that lately. I'm trying to teach my daughter the importance of independence. I want her to be able to take control of her life.

Interviewer: How old is your daughter?

Marielena: She just turned 12.

Interview: Isn't she a little young to think about being independent?

Marielena: No, I don't think so. See, I think she faces too much pressure in her life. There's a lot of pressure to do well in school, and my parents have high expectations for the children in my family. They want the children to become professionals, you know, lawyers or architects, that sort of thing. I think all those high expectations put children under too much stress. As my daughter grows up, I want her to realize that she has options.

Interviewer: Some people say that parents should have high expectations of their children. Wouldn't you agree with that?

Marielena: No, not really. I think there are **many** ways to be happy and productive, so I think people should have choices. I want my daughter to be good at something that is meaningful for **her**, something that will make **her** happy. Maybe she'll become an artist — a painter, a singer, an actress, or a chef! What's important is that she make her own decisions.

Interviewer: What if she can't find a job being an actress or a chef?

Marielena: Well, she can do something else. I have a friend who's in his late 30s. He was working in a hospital, but he didn't like it. He just went back to college because he decided he wants to be a lawyer. And nobody told him he shouldn't do it. Even though, you know, it **is** a little bit strange - he's one of the oldest students in the class. And he's sitting there with 18 year olds! (laughs) But that's OK. You **can** change professions, you know, no matter how old you are. After all, he's only in his thirties!

Interviewer: That's interesting. Well now, Dan, let me ask you the same question. What are some values that are important to you?

Dan: Well, the first thing I think of is hard work. And self-reliance. These values are everywhere you look. For example, politicians are always talking about the value of personal responsibility.

Interviewer: Is personal responsibility the same as self-reliance?

Dan: Yeah, you know, depending on yourself and trying to improve yourself. I don't think you should grow up expecting other people to take care of you. And you know, that is common-sense advice, especially in **this** economic climate.

Interviewer: You've just started college, right?

Dan: Yes. And I take college really seriously. That's because I know that if I want to do well, I have to study hard. So I put a lot of effort into my studies. Oh, and I have a part-time job, too. I also just started working at a bookstore, and I really **like** having a job. I mean, obviously, sometimes it's hard to have to go to work instead of watching TV or going out with your friends (laughs). But once I get there, I feel like I'm doing something with my life.

Interviewer: Oh, really? You work as well as study?

Dan: Yeah, I think that working helps you to prepare for life after college. Having a job helps you to set goals and work toward them. And I also see work as my duty and my obligation. I don't want to keep asking my family for money — I like having my own spending money. That way, I can do whatever I like with it.

Listening for tone of voice, page 133

CD2 TR17 **Excerpt 1**

Marielena: "I think there are **many** ways to be happy and productive, so I think people should have choices. I want my daughter to be good at something that is meaningful for **her**, something that will make **her** happy."

Excerpt 2

Marielena: "It **is** a little bit strange — he's one of the oldest students in the class. And he's sitting there with 18-year-olds! (laughs) But that's OK. You **can** change professions, you know, no matter how old you. After all, he's only in his thirties!"

Excerpt 3

Dan: "I don't think you should grow up expecting other people to take care o f you. And you know, that is common-sense advice. Especially in **this** economic climate."

Excerpt 4

Dan: "I also just started working at a bookstore, and I really **like** having a job. I mean, obviously, sometimes it's hard to have to go to work instead of watching TV or going out with your friends (laughs). But once I get there, I feel like I'm doing something with my life."

Interview 2: Values in Theory and Practice

CD2 TR18 **Listening for main ideas,** page 134

Interviewer: Hello, Pauline. Values… how important are they to you?

Pauline: Yeah, well, people talk a lot about values, but I think you have to see what happens in practice. In real life.

Interviewer: What do you mean?

Pauline: Well, you know, everyone says it's important to be independent. And I think independence IS an important value. But being independent shouldn't mean that you know, you go off on your own, you don't need anyone else. . . . It isn't the same as being cold, or distant. And I think a lot of people *are* cold and distant. For example, I've lived in other countries where there is a lot of contact with neighbors. And people hang out on the street and talk about everything that's going on. But where I live, nobody even knows who their neighbors are. There are eight apartments on my floor, but I've only ever seen one or two neighbors. We say "Good morning," maybe even "Have a nice day." But that's it. People are so unfriendly.

Interviewer: What about other values?

Pauline: Oh, this is interesting. I was reading the other day that modern society values extroverts more than introverts. And I think that is true. Like at work, everyone is very aggressive. And we're expected to go to team meetings every morning and say what we think. My boss told everyone that they had to be assertive. If you go to a team meeting and don't say anything, then they think you're not making any contributions.

Interviewer: Why do you have a problem with that?

Pauline: Well, even though I'm not exactly a quiet person, I do like to think before I speak. So sometimes I'll be in a meeting, and I don't say anything because I need more time to think things through. That happened to me the other day. And then my boss put me on the spot. He said, "Pauline, don't you have any comments?" And I was pretty embarrassed. I couldn't think of what to say right then and there. I need more time to think sometimes. But that doesn't mean I'm not a team player.

Interviewer: So, you've talked about independence and extroversion. Can you add anything else?

Pauline: Hmm. Well, a third thing is informality. Americans are pretty informal, and I am too. Like, when I was in school, we got to call our teachers by their first name. It was never Mr. or Mrs. so and so — we called them Dave and Margaret, for example.

Interviewer: So do you agree with being informal?

Pauline: Yes, I do, but you *can* take it a bit too far. For example, I went to the opera the other day, and I saw guys wearing jeans. I think that's unbelievable. Americans wear jeans everywhere they go. I think men should wear something more formal if they're going to the opera or out to a nice restaurant — you know, not a hat or a suit, but at least a tie and a jacket. It's a matter of respect. Of course, you want to be comfortable, but I do think there's a limit.

Lecture: Harry Peterson, "Three American Folk Heroes"

 **CD2 TR19 Before the Lecture: Listening for key words,** page 138

1. Today I'm going to talk about three traditional American folk heroes. And by folk heroes, I mean real people or imaginary figures who do extraordinary things or who have extraordinary powers.

2. So, let's begin with the cowboy. Think about all the places you see cowboys. If you turn on the TV, I guarantee you'll find a cowboy movie on one of the channels. And the image of the cowboy is also seen constantly in advertising and fashion.

3. An entrepreneur is a person who starts a company — who makes business deals in order to make a profit. We think of entrepreneurs as people who have great ideas and take risks. And the entrepreneur is also a very powerful symbol of American values.

4. There are all kinds of superheroes — Superman, Batman, Wonder Woman, and so on. Most superheroes have extraordinary powers, even though they are in some ways very human.

Lecture Part 1: "Cowboys and Entrepreneurs"

Clarifying your notes, page 140

CD2 TR20 Good afternoon, everyone. Today I'm going to talk about three traditional American folk heroes. And by folk heroes, I mean real people or imaginary figures who do extraordinary things or who have extraordinary powers. The United States, like every country, has many of these traditional folk heroes, but I want to talk about three famous ones, and they are the cowboy, the entrepreneur, and the superhero. In this country, we see these three images everywhere — in the media, in advertising. . . . They represent some of our most important values, and I think that's why they're so popular.

So, let's begin with the cowboy. Think about all the places you see cowboys. If you turn on the TV, I guarantee you'll find a cowboy movie on one of the channels. And the image of the cowboy is also seen constantly in advertising and fashion.

In fact, I bet that 90 percent of the people in this room are probably wearing jeans.

Why do you think the cowboy is such a popular image in our culture? Well, let's go back in history about 150 years. During the nineteenth century, people began moving west in order to make their fortune. Some of these settlers started large cattle ranches and hired cowboys. Over time the cowboy became a classic American hero. Think about it: The cowboy works alone, in difficult weather and dangerous conditions. He is completely self-reliant. He never seems to need money or anything like that. He represents courage, freedom, and independence — qualities that almost all Americans still value today.

OK, so next, let's go on to talk about the entrepreneur. An entrepreneur is a person who starts a company — who makes business deals in order to make a profit. We think of entrepreneurs as people who have great ideas and take risks. And the entrepreneur is also a very powerful symbol of American values. That's because entrepreneurs represent the idea that if you're smart, if you work hard, and if you have good ideas, you can succeed. This kind of success story has been popular ever since the Horatio Alger stories of the early twentieth century. And although many young Americans have never heard of Horatio Alger, they certainly know of Steve Jobs or other successful people who have become American heroes because of their talent, their belief in themselves, and the risks that they take.

Now, the last American hero I'd like you to think about is imaginary. I'm talking about the kind of superhero found in comic books, movies, and television. There are all kinds of superheroes: Superman, Batman, Wonder Woman, and so on. Most superheroes have extraordinary powers even though they are in some ways very human. Superheroes appeal to our deepest fantasies and desires. They're fast and they're powerful, but they have a strong sense of right and wrong. Superman, for example, is always defending the good guys and punishing the bad guys. Most Americans relate very strongly to the values that the superhero represents, and that's why they are so popular in our culture.

Lecture Part 2: "Questions and Answers"

 Taking notes on questions and answers, page 141

CD2 TR21 **Lecturer:** All right, are there any questions?

Student 1: Professor Peterson, can you explain a little more about entrepreneurs? Are they always very successful?

Lecturer: Well, some of them aren't successful; others are. But after the Civil War, there was a period of huge industrial expansion in the United States. Thousands of miles of railroads were built and that made it possible for industries like steel and oil to grow. And since that time there have been some entrepreneurs who have been very, very successful and become extremely rich. Have you heard of, uh, let's see, Andrew Carnegie? He made millions of dollars from his steel factories. Oh, and I bet you've heard of John D. Rockefeller. He made his fortune in oil. Carnegie and Rockefeller were two of our earliest entrepreneur-heroes. Another question?

Student 2: Are there any more modern entrepreneurs that have this "hero quality" you've been describing?

Lecturer: Sure! A couple people come to mind. In addition to Steve Jobs, the brilliant CEO of Apple, I can think of Bill Gates, the co-founder of Microsoft, and Mark Zuckerberg, the Internet entrepreneur. The most amazing thing is that these men all exemplify a lot of the values we've already spoken about. They're seen as people who have the personal qualities that guarantee success.

Student 3: I'm really interested in where these values come from, so can you talk a bit more about Superman? Did the Superman figure come out in the nineteenth century?

Lecturer: No, the first Superman comic book was written a little later, in the 1930s, and the other superhero characters came after that. One after another after another! Have you seen X-Men or Batman? They come out with one sequel after the other. Movies about superheroes are some of the most profitable movies in history! It seems like Americans never get tired of the superhero image. Incidentally, let's not forget the James Bond films. They're British, of course, but they've been coming out since the 1960s, and they also communicate similar values.

Student 4: Professor, I have a question. You didn't mention almost any women folk heroes. Why not?

Lecturer: Well, yes, I thought about that. The thing is, there are very few traditional folk heroes who are women. There was a woman named Annie Oakley in the nineteenth century who was famous for her shooting skills. At a time when most women were wives and mothers, she traveled around and had shooting competitions with men. Also, she gave a lot of the money she made to different charities. And then there's Wonder Woman, as I said before, the comic book superhero. She first appeared in 1941. But most of the traditional folk heroes have been men, although I would hope that's going to change in the future.

🔊 Unit 4: American Values
CD2
TR22
Chapter 8: American Values Today

Getting Started:
Listening for specific information, page 146

Woman: I've just been reading this article about Generation Y. That's you, isn't it?

Man: Yeah, I think so. That's the same as the Millennial Generation, right? I was born in 1990. So what does the article say about me?

Woman: Well, it says there are about 80 million Generation Ys in America. That's a lot. It's about 20 percent of the population! Generation Y is about six times as big as Generation X, which is the generation that came right before. There are . . . let's see . . . 79 million Baby Boomers. So the Millennials, or Generation Y, is about the same size as the Boomers.

Man: What else does the article say?

Woman: It talks about the values of your generation.

Man: Like what?

Woman: Well, for example, it says you have a tolerance for diversity. It says Generation Ys are very open and tolerant. And then . . . now this is interesting, you like speed and constant change. You're the Internet generation, so you don't like to wait for things.

Man: That's true. What else?

Woman: It says you value independence and social responsibility! Is that true?

Man: Yeah, I think we do. I think we should do what we can to make the world a better place.

🔊 **Interview 1: Differences in Values Between**
CD2
TR23 **Parents and Children**
Drawing inferences, page 148

Interviewer: Rosiane, do you think that your own values are very different from the values of your parents?

Rosiane: Oh, yeah, I think they are different. My parents have very traditional values. Like they wanted me to meet a nice guy, get married when I was about 20 and have kids, so that they could help bring up the grandchildren. But I didn't really want to do that.

Interviewer: What did you want?

Rosiane: Well, I guess I was more adventurous. When I was in my early 20s, I wasn't looking for a **husband** — I was busy looking for a **career**. I studied hard, and then I became an accountant. It took me a long time to reach that point. I'm 33 now and just recently got married, so I don't have any kids yet.

Interviewer: What do your parents think about your choices?

Rosiane: Well, even though my values are different from theirs, they accepted my decisions.

Interviewer: Benjamin, how about you?

Benjamin: Well, I think I see eye to eye with my parents on many general values, like respect, cooperation, family . . . But I guess my parents and I disagree about how that works out in practice.

Interviewer: What do you mean?

Benjamin: Well, see, I respect my parents' **opinions**, but they need to respect my **privacy**. Look, even though I'm in college now, my mother's always calling me. She's like, "Did you do your homework, honey?" "Did you have dinner yet?" And my father will call, too and ask me, "Did you speak to your professor?" "Did you choose your courses for next semester?" They call that being a "helicopter parent." Perhaps that's a kind of pejorative expression, and I don't mean to insult my parents. It's just that . . . well, your parents don't need to keep constantly hovering over you. Helicopter parents keep constantly hovering over you, like they're in a helicopter watching what you do from the air. They won't leave you alone.

Interviewer: Oh, so you don't want them to be so involved?

Benjamin: Well, I like them being involved in my life, but they should leave me alone a little more. They're kind of . . . too involved. And it doesn't stop in college, either! They keep giving my older brother advice about his job, and he's in his mid-thirties. He's been working for ten years already!

Interviewer: Oh, I see! Well, thank you, Benjamin. Now, Christine, are your values different from your parents' values?

Christine: Well, my parents are more conservative than I am. **I'm** really open to change, but they **aren't**. My parents and my whole family all live in the same town, and no one has ever moved away. You know, my parents have never even been out of the country.

Interviewer: Never?

Christine: No, in fact, my mom's only been on a plane three times.

Interviewer: And have you been out of the country?

Christine: Well, yeah. I mean, I've already traveled to lots of different places. And I lived abroad for a while. I think it's really important to travel because traveling makes you more open-minded. I like meeting new people, I don't know, experimenting with new things. I like having that kind of freedom.

Interviewer: And what about your friends? Do most of them feel the same way?

Christine: Yeah, most of my friends feel the same way. They don't live in the same places as their parents. They move around because they're exploring and trying to see how they can improve their lives.

Listening for stressed words, page 149

CD2 TR24 **Excerpt 1**

Rosiane: When I was in my early 20s, I wasn't looking for a **husband** — I was busy looking for a **career**.

Excerpt 2

Benjamin: I respect my parents' **opinions**, but they need to respect my **privacy**.

Excerpt 3

Christine: I'm really open to change, but they **aren't**.

Interview 2: Values in the Workplace

CD2 TR25 ### Listening for specific information, page 150

Interviewer: Hi, Sandra. I wanted to interview you because I know you have strong opinions about the values young people need in the workplace.

Sandra: This is true. I'm a business professor, and I'm always giving advice to my students about the kind of values they have to develop in order to succeed. I ask my students, "If you had your own business, would you hire you?"

Interviewer: What values do you think they need?

Sandra: Well, the first thing they need to learn is the value of time. You know what they say: "Time is money." I find that sometimes, students don't respect deadlines. They think, "Well, I don't have to submit my paper on time — it doesn't matter if it's a day or two late," or they arrive for class five minutes after it starts. But they have to learn that that is not acceptable. So I give them an example: Suppose you want to buy a car, and the dealer tells you that the car will be ready Friday at three o'clock in the afternoon. And you go to the dealer, and everything is all paid for — you've paid your deposit and so on. But the dealer tells you, "Well no, I'm sorry, you won't be able to get your car until next Friday." What is your reaction? You're going to be really upset.

Interviewer: Of course, I can see that. Time is money! What other values are important?

Sandra: Well, after time, the second value is cooperation. Working as a team. And this is a very difficult value for a lot of my students to learn. They want to be individuals. They want to work alone and show what they can do. They want to stand out. But that is not what we do in the workplace. You don't work in isolation.

Interviewer: But don't you think individual effort is important?

Sandra: Yes, of course it's always important to do your best, but I'd say cooperation is even more important.

Interviewer: And what else?

Sandra: Well, the third value is professionalism. What I mean is, have a professional attitude. You should dress, speak, and write in an appropriate way, depending on the situation. See, I believe you should behave professionally at work. And when you speak or write, you should be careful to use a formal tone, especially with customers.

Lecture: Jason LaRose, "Conservative and Liberal Values in American Politics"

CD2 TR26 ### Before the Lecture: Listening for general statements, page 156

1. But even though people's values are very diverse, the strongest voices in American politics today do generally fall into two groups: conservative and liberal.

2. Conservatives usually put a strong emphasis on personal responsibility.

3. Most liberals, on the other hand, think the government should be very active in fixing social problems like poverty and illness.

4. Generally, conservatives think government is too big and expensive.

5. Conservatives typically believe the government should stay out of the way of business.

6. But in general, liberals believe that government should control and regulate business through strict laws or taxes.

Lecture Part 1: "Conservative and Liberal Values"

Taking notes in a point-by-point format, page 157

CD2
TR27

Good morning, everyone. The focus today will be conservative and liberal values in American politics. Of course, you have to understand that I can only talk about these things in a general way today, because this is a very broad topic. It's very hard to make specific statements about Americans' political beliefs since there are more than 300 million Americans from so many different racial, religious, and economic backgrounds. But even though people's values are very diverse, the strongest voices in American politics today do generally fall into two groups: conservative and liberal. So let me outline for you some of the basic differences between conservatives and liberals in three areas: the role of government, taxes, and government regulation of business.

Let's begin with the role of government. Conservatives usually put a strong emphasis on personal responsibility. They think that people should be responsible for themselves. In other words, they don't believe it's the government's responsibility to pay for social programs that guarantee things like a minimum wage or health insurance. Most liberals, on the other hand, think the government should be very active in fixing social problems like poverty and illness. Liberals believe it's the responsibility of the government to provide money and help for people who are poor or sick. So for example, they typically support laws that guarantee workers a minimum wage or free lunches at school for poor children.

Now let's move to the second difference I wanted to mention. Generally, conservatives think government is too big and expensive. A big government requires citizens to pay high taxes to support its programs. And, high taxes are not popular with conservatives, especially during economic recessions. Conservatives are in favor of cutting taxes for the rich as a way of stimulating job creation and economic growth. But liberals believe taxes are necessary because they help government provide the services we need, uh, for an equal and productive society. Taxes are important because they give government money to support social programs like the ones I mentioned before. OK?

Finally, conservatives typically believe the government should stay out of the way of business, that it shouldn't interfere too much in the way business works. They think that an economy with less government control is the best way for the economy to grow and to provide jobs. But in general, liberals believe that government should control and regulate business through strict laws or taxes, because if it doesn't, they think entrepreneurs won't care about their workers, their customers, or the environment. They'll only care about their own profits. So, many liberals think business should be closely regulated, and they favor establishing government programs as a way of stimulating employment opportunities during economic recessions.

Lecture Part 2: "Values and Political Parties"

Using information on the board to help you take notes, page 159

CD2
TR28

Let me remind you that the U.S. has two main political parties, so in an election, voters generally choose between the Republicans and the Democrats. And in general I think most people associate the Republican Party with conservative values and ideas, and the Democratic Party with liberal ones. But people's values can change over time, and we can see this clearly if we look at the results of the presidential elections of 1964, 1980, 2000, and 2008.

Can you all see the board? What you'll notice immediately is that there has been a noticeable change in the voting patterns over the past 40-something years. In 1964, a majority of votes — about 61 percent — were for the Democratic candidate for president, Lyndon Johnson. Sixteen years later, in 1980, more than 50 percent of the votes went to the Republican candidate, Ronald Reagan. Reagan won by nearly 60 percent when he ran for a second term four years later. In 2000, the voters were more equally divided. In fact, the country was split down the middle — about half voted for Republican candidate George W. Bush, and half for the Democratic candidate, Al Gore. In the end, the Republicans won that year, but the results were very, very close. Then, in 2008, the Democratic Party again won the national elections, with 53 percent of the vote. The situation in 2012 was similar. In that election, Barack Obama won his reelection campaign, but only by the slimmest of margins.

Why do changes like these happen? How do we explain them? Well, sometimes changes in voting patterns are the result of economic conditions, meaning, for example, that voters are responding to high employment, or unemployment rates. A strong economy helped Ronald

Reagan get elected for a second term in 1984, for example. Or, there could be other reasons, such as concern about the international situation. The attack of September 11, 2001, was probably a factor in George W. Bush's reelection in 2004. But obviously, a third reason for changing voting patterns is that a new generation of voters have different values from the generation that came before them. Millennials don't necessarily vote the same way as their parents, the Baby Boomers. And people's values often change as they get older and they tend to become more conservative. On the other hand, as more young people participate in elections, the strength of the Democratic Party tends to increase. This was evident in 2008 in the election of Barack Obama.

I want to emphasize that I've been discussing American political values and the political system in a very general way. In practice, many Americans are not strict conservatives or liberals; they may have conservative beliefs on some issues and liberal ideas on others. And all Democrats and Republicans are not the same, either. You know, often we see our country divided on the map between red and blue states. But in my opinion, all 50 states are actually different shades of purple because there are both conservative and liberal voters in every state in the nation.